Getting On Track With English

the complete set of worksheets
and word lists for the student

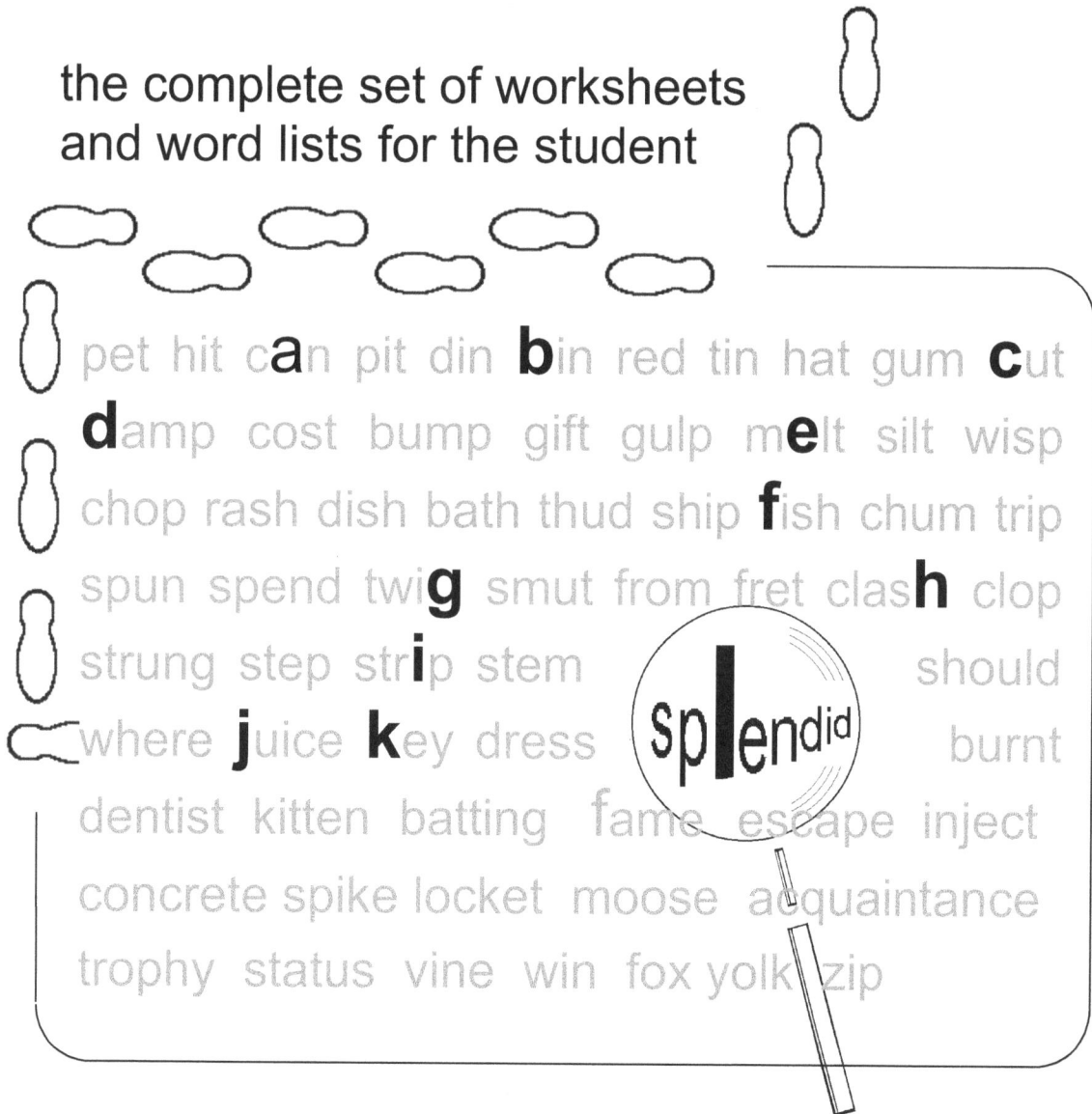

pet hit c**a**n pit din **b**in red tin hat gum **c**ut
damp cost bump gift gulp m**e**lt silt wisp
chop rash dish bath thud ship **f**ish chum trip
spun spend twi**g** smut from fret clas**h** clop
strung step str**i**p stem   should
where **j**uice **k**ey dress   sp**l**en^did   burnt
dentist kitten batting fame escape inject
concrete spike locket moose acquaintance
trophy status vine win fox yolk zip

Maureen Cox

Canadian ISBN 978-1-987926-24-8

The rights of Maureen Cox to be identified as the author of this Work have been asserted by her in accordance with the Copyright, Designs and Patents Act   1988.

All enquiries regarding this edition to:

Mimast Inc
Arnhem Road
Duncan BC
Canada
email: mimast.inc@gmail.com

Worksheets Nos. 1 to 27

1. One syllable words with a short vowel: (ă) (ĕ) (ĭ) (ŏ) (ŭ) ☐
2. Words with final consonant blends:
   -ct -ft -ld -lf -lm -lp -lt -mp -nd -nt -pt -sp -st ☐
3. Words with initial consonant blends:
   cr- fr- pl- sl- sm- sp- tr- tw- ☐
4. Words with initial consonant blends:
   bl- cl- dr- fl- gl- gr- pr- sn- sw- ☐
5. Words with initial consonant blends:
   br- sc- scr- shr- spl- spr- st- str- ☐
6. Words with consonant digraphs:
   (ch) (ng) (sh) (t̶h̶) (th) ☐
7. Irregular words ☐
8. Words ending in ff, ll, ss and zz ☐
9. The sounds of (är), (ôr) and (er) ☐
10. Two syllable words with two short vowels ☐
11. Two syllable words where the middle consonant is doubled ☐
12. Silent 'e' ☐
13. The sounds of ($\overline{ee}$), ($\overline{oo}$) and ($\breve{oo}$) ☐
14. Words with the (k) sound spelt c-, k-, -c, -ck and -k ☐
15. The final (s) sound spelt -ce, -se and -ss ☐
16. Stable final syllables:
    -ble -dle -fle -gle -ple -stle -tle -zle ☐
17. Stable final syllables: -cal -ckle -cle -kle ☐
18. The sound of (ā) spelt ai and ay ☐
19. The sounds of (ō) spelt oa and ow and of (ou) spelt ou and ow ☐
20. The sounds of (ē), (ĕ) and (ā) spelt ea ☐
21. Words with au and aw ☐
22. The sound of (ū) spelt eu, ew and ue ☐
23. Words with the (j) sound spelt j-, g-, -dge and -ge ☐
24. The sound of (f) spelt f, -ff and ph ☐
25. The final (ŭs) sound spelt -us, -ous and -ious ☐
26. The sound of (shŭn) spelt -tion, -sion, -ssion and -cian ☐
27. Words often misspelt ☐

WORKSHEET 1

Name: _____ Date: _____

a b c d e f g h i j k l m n o p q r s t u v w x y z

pet hat bed hit cat big dog cot leg bit bun fun rug
can hen tin hug jam bin box fat kit hop log mop cup
run top quit net but red sit mug man pen vet pin hut
not win yes fox ten sun yet bus van zip wet

☐ Circle or cross out each letter of the alphabet in sequence

☐ Read aloud and colour each group of short vowel words

☐ Find three more examples of each short vowel sound

(ă)	(ĕ)	(ĭ)	(ŏ)	(ŭ)
hat	net	win	mop	sun

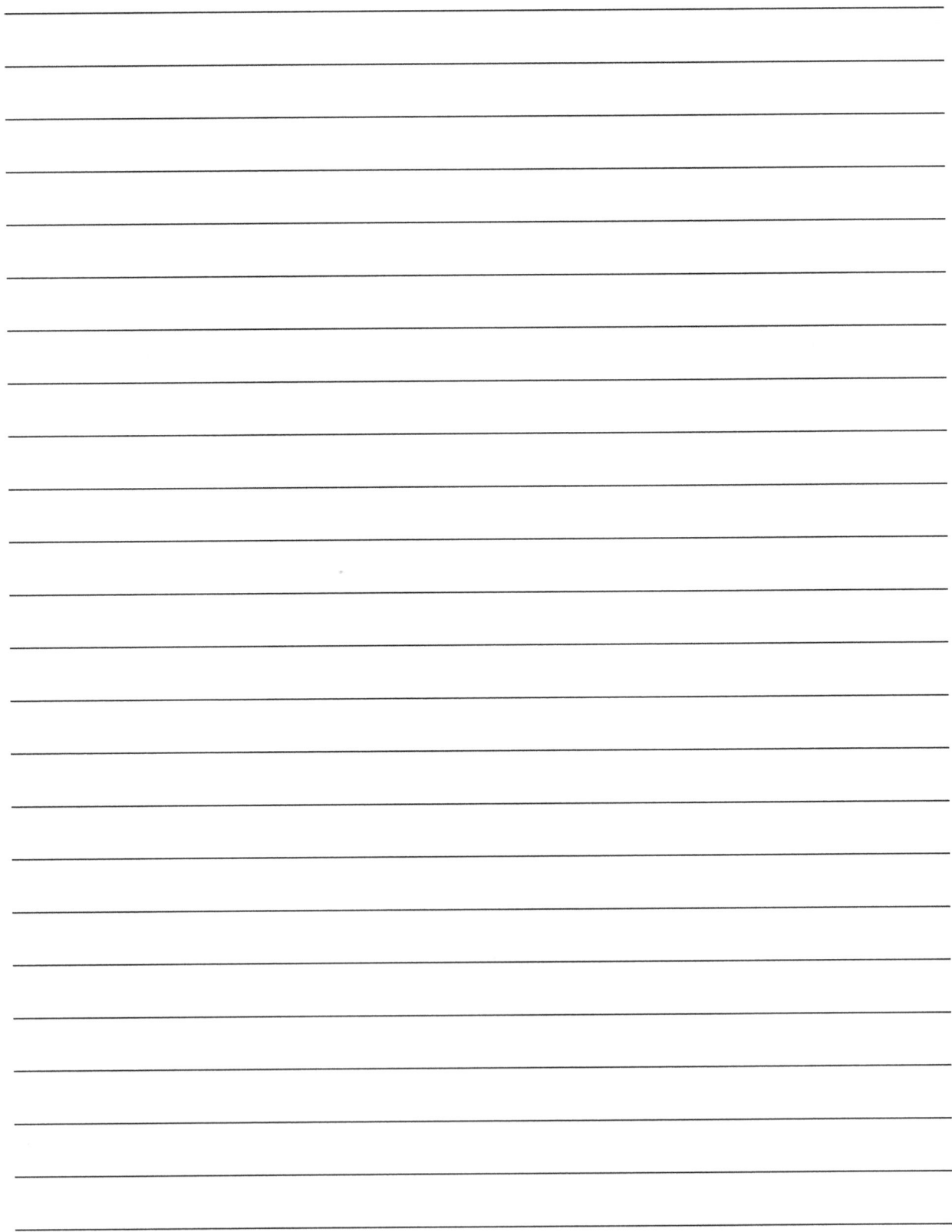

WORKSHEET 2

Name: _____   Date: _____

a b c d e f g h i j k l m n o p q r s t u v w x y z

and elf dust bold cost belt gold act end felt help golf
fact hand gift jump gasp hint kilt soft camp kept hold
calf pond film lift lamp told tact melt wept quilt test
raft nest land elm must helm lost vest tent sand west
exact went yelp zest wind

☐ Circle or cross out each letter of the alphabet in sequence

☐ Read aloud and colour each group of final consonant blends

☐ Find one example of each final consonant blend.

-ct	_____	-mp	_____
-ft	_____	-nd	_____
-ld	_____	-nt	_____
-lf	_____	-pt	_____
-lm	_____	-sp	_____
-lp	_____	-st	_____
-lt	_____		

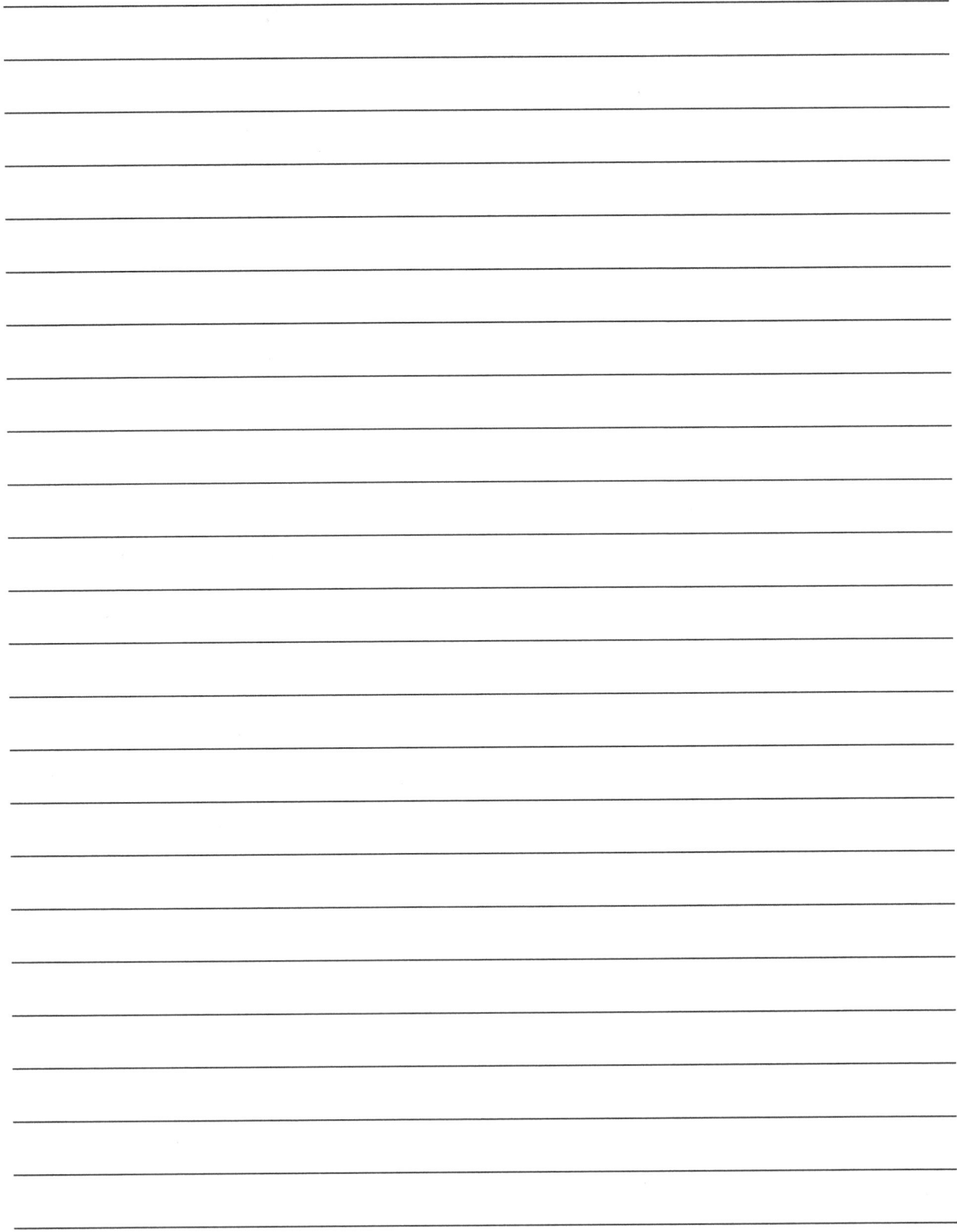

WORKSHEET 3

Name: _____ Date: _____

a b c d e f g h i j k l m n o p q r s t u v w x y z

span smug crib trap trim crab fret from slid trip spun spend frog smut crush twig jog-trot trick trod crop spit plan spin smog twin smash tram slot slim twenty plaque slit trust plug fresh frost travel French plod twist crux plot slip cry spot slug cram crag plum crazy

☐ Circle or cross out each letter of the alphabet in sequence

☐ Read aloud and colour each group of consonant blends

☐ Find one example of each initial consonant blend.

cr- _____   sm- _____

fr- _____   sp- _____

pl- _____   tr- _____

sl- _____   tw- _____

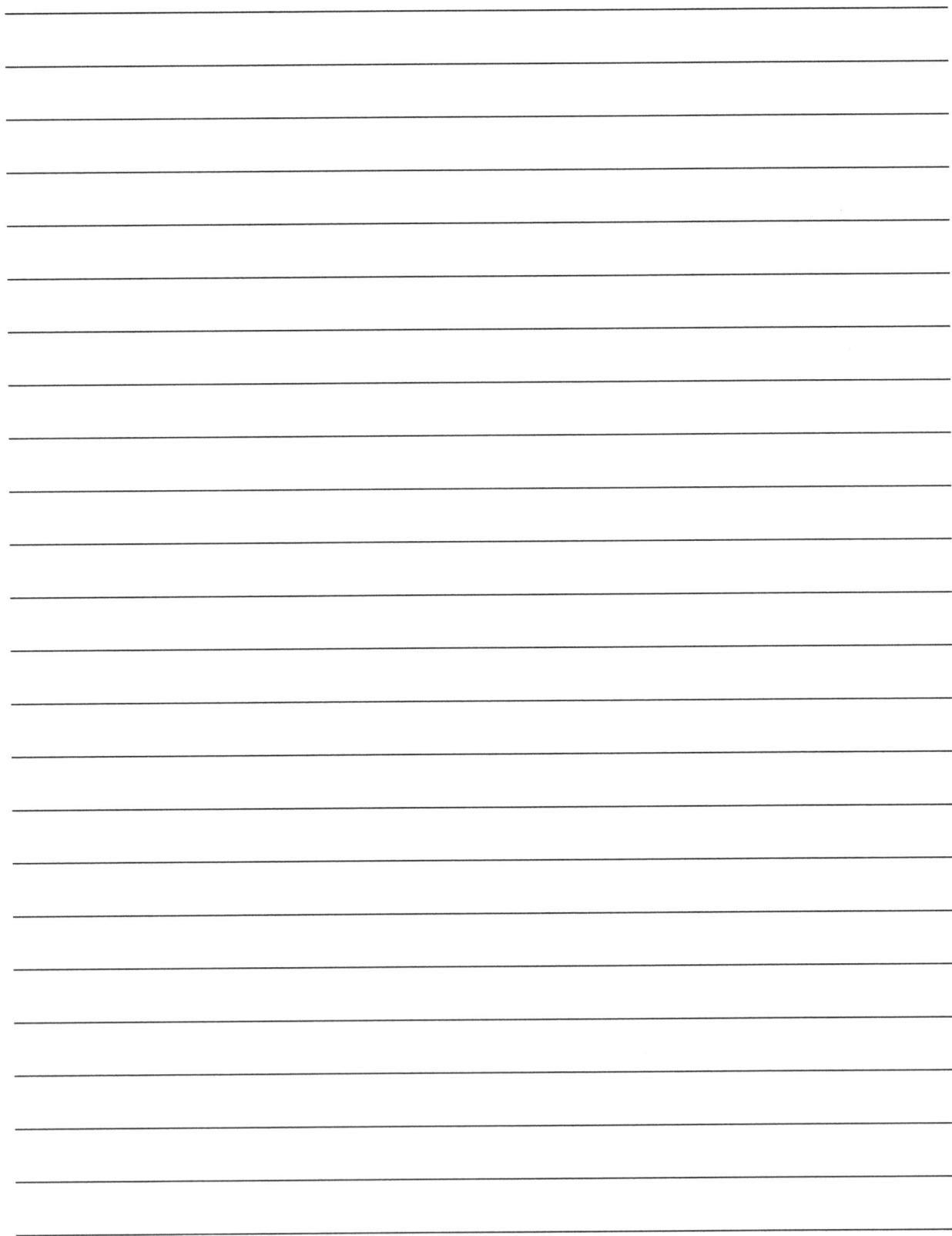

WORKSHEET 4

Name: _____   Date: _____

a b c d e f g h i j k l m n o p q r s t u v w x y z

glad grub snip snag clap drab grim fled flap glen
clash clop grid pram jet-black swag drum clog drank
swum clip prop clan prod snap flag clef clique grip
flop glut swam drip clot gland drop snub glove snug
glum flat snob prim swim flax dry blot flan
Switzerland swig

☐ Circle or cross out each letter of the alphabet in sequence

☐ Read aloud and colour each group of consonant blends

☐ Write in each box one example of the consonant blend

bl- _____   gl- _____

cl- _____   gr- _____

dr- _____   pr- _____

fl- _____   sn- _____

sw- _____

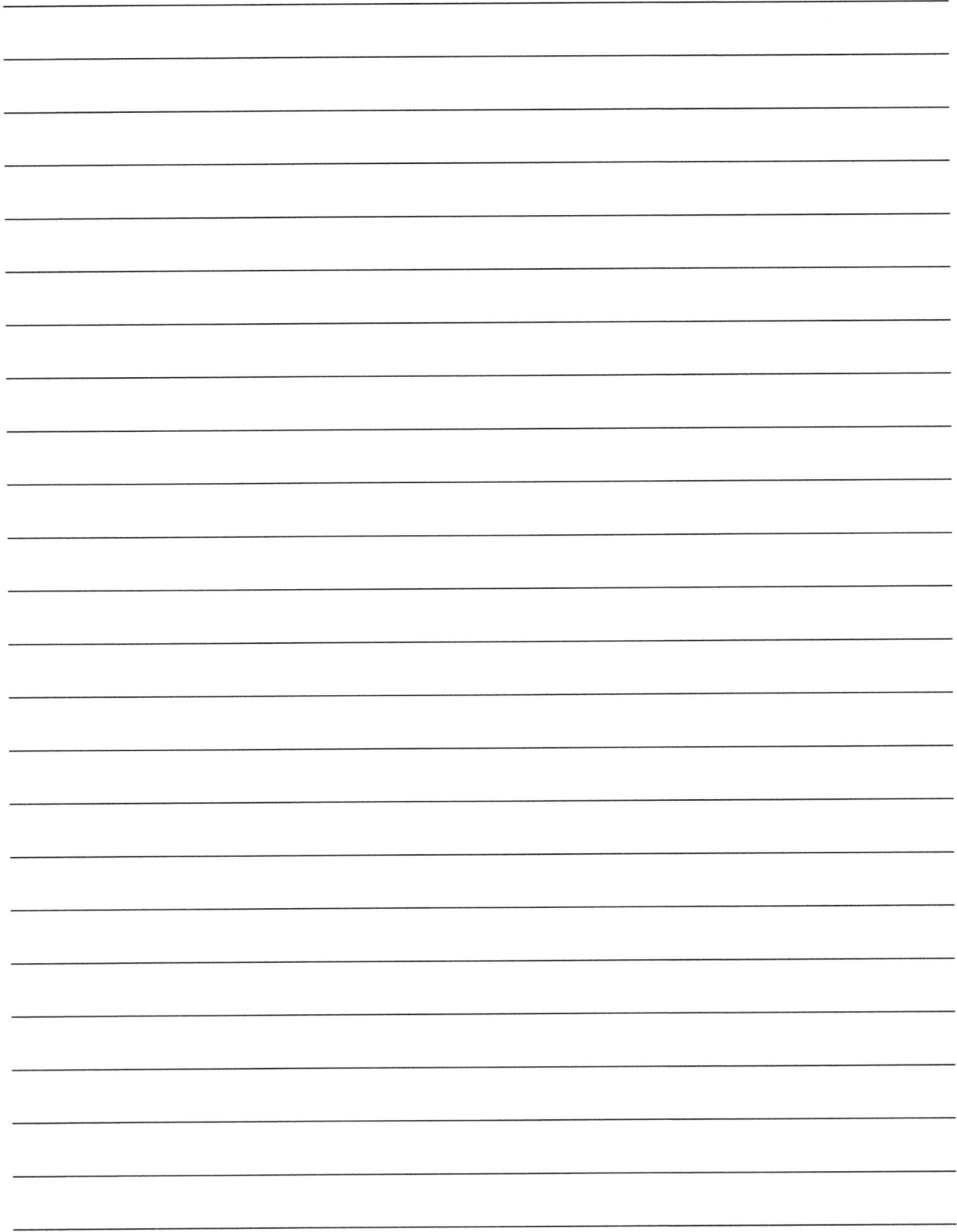

WORKSHEET 5

Name: _____   Date: _____

a b c d e f g h i j k l m n o p q r s t u v w x y z

strong split sprat stub strap strip scrum stud scrub
script shred stab shrift strand stump strung step stem
shrimp steeple-jack splash shrink scrap scan scram
sprint stag stop brusque strum strut sprig spring
shrivel scrimp shrub brew scamp splint scum
strongbox shrug sting sty stamp brim stilt stanza stunt
sprang

☐ Circle or cross out each letter of the alphabet in sequence

☐ Read aloud and colour each group of consonant blends

☐ Write in each box one example of the consonant blend

br- _____   spl- _____

sc- _____   spr- _____

scr- _____   st- _____

shr- _____   str- _____

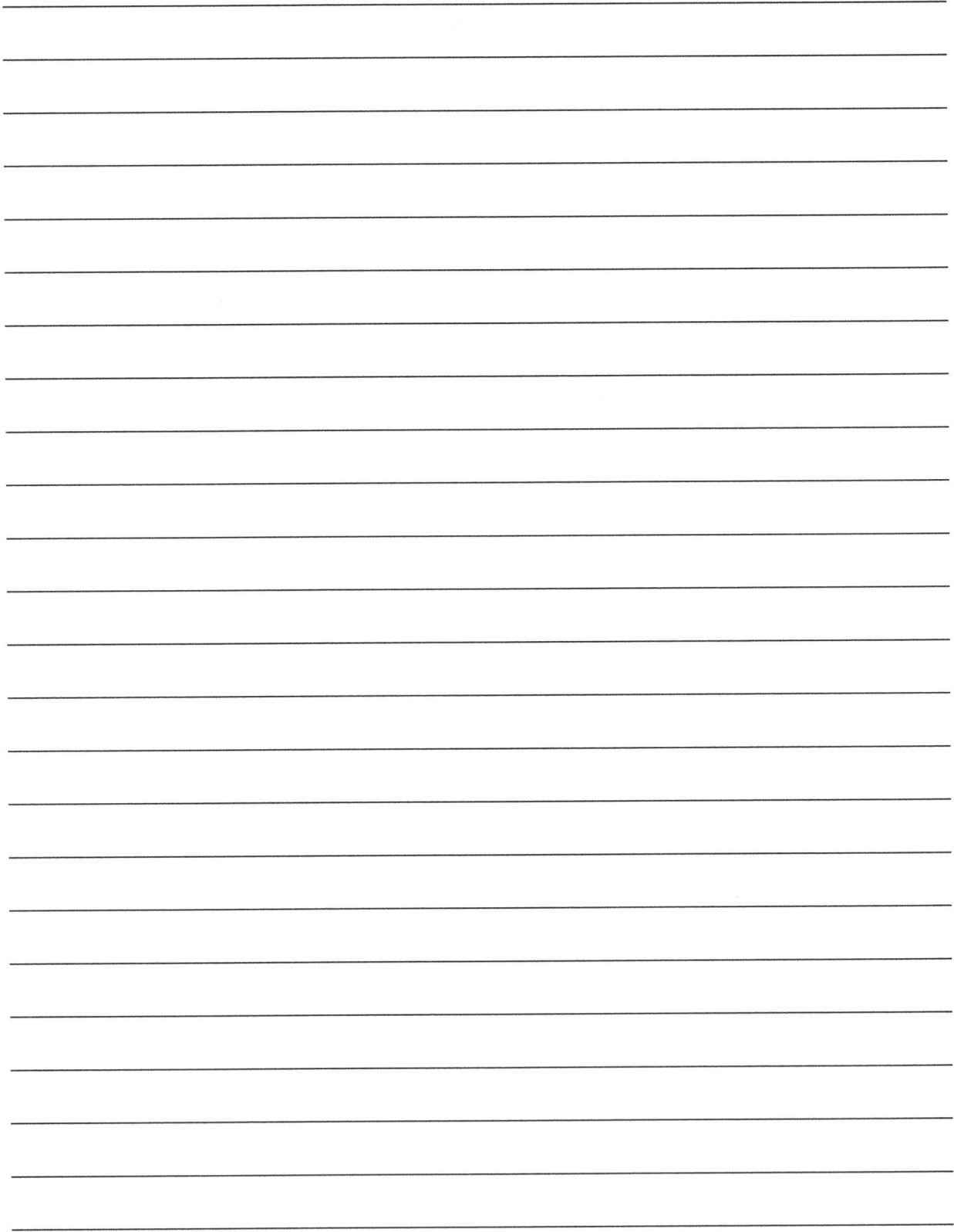

WORKSHEET 6

Name: _____   Date: _____

a b c d e f g h i j k l m n o p q r s t u v w x y z

sang chip bath chat dish chop bunch the this shut fish ring then rang inch Joshua long king sing ship lunch cash them song theft moth thin pinch that mother quench shop rich thud thing shed chin wing father lung path vanish munch with hush mixing rash wish Thursday zither

☐ Circle or cross out each letter of the alphabet in sequence

☐ Read aloud and colour each group of digraphs

☐ Find three more examples of each digraph

(ch)	(ng)	(sh)	(t̶h̶)	(th)
rich	sing	shut	them	thing

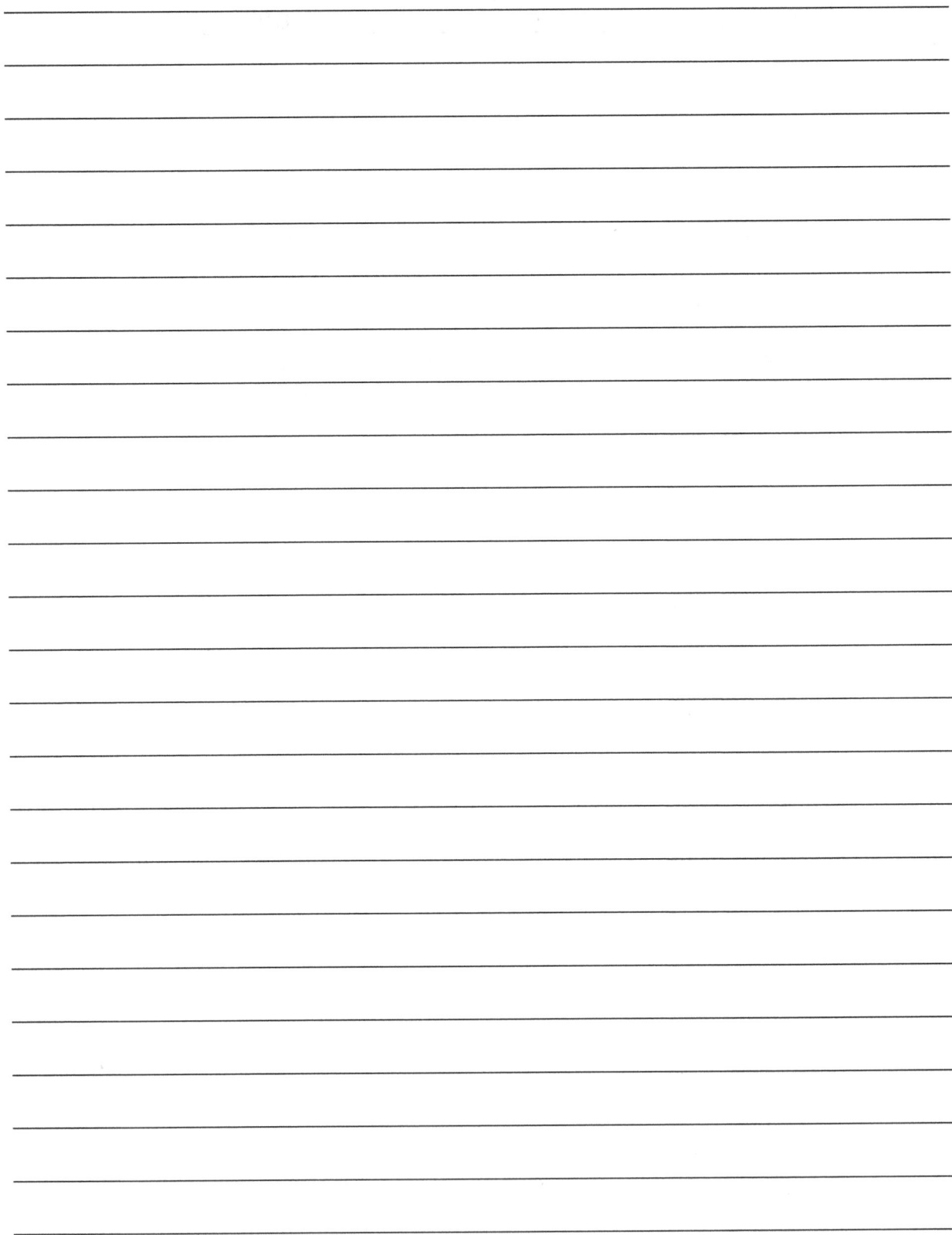

WORKSHEET 7

Name: _____   Date: _____

a b c d e f g h i j k l m n o p q r s t u v w x y z

when was there because three do which saw eight what friend want give they too island where juice key for should two come once some put could does query who witch of toes four beautiful have any would seven their you your xylophone were said one are tzar many why

☐ Cross out each letter of the alphabet in sequence

☐ Read all the words aloud

☐ Cross out the incorrect words in the boxes

I go | to/too/two | a good school. My | to/too/two | brothers go | their/there |

| to/too/two. | I have | for/four | friends. I do not know | which/witch |

| one/won | I like the best. Mum says | thay/they | can all | come/cum |

| for/four | tea.

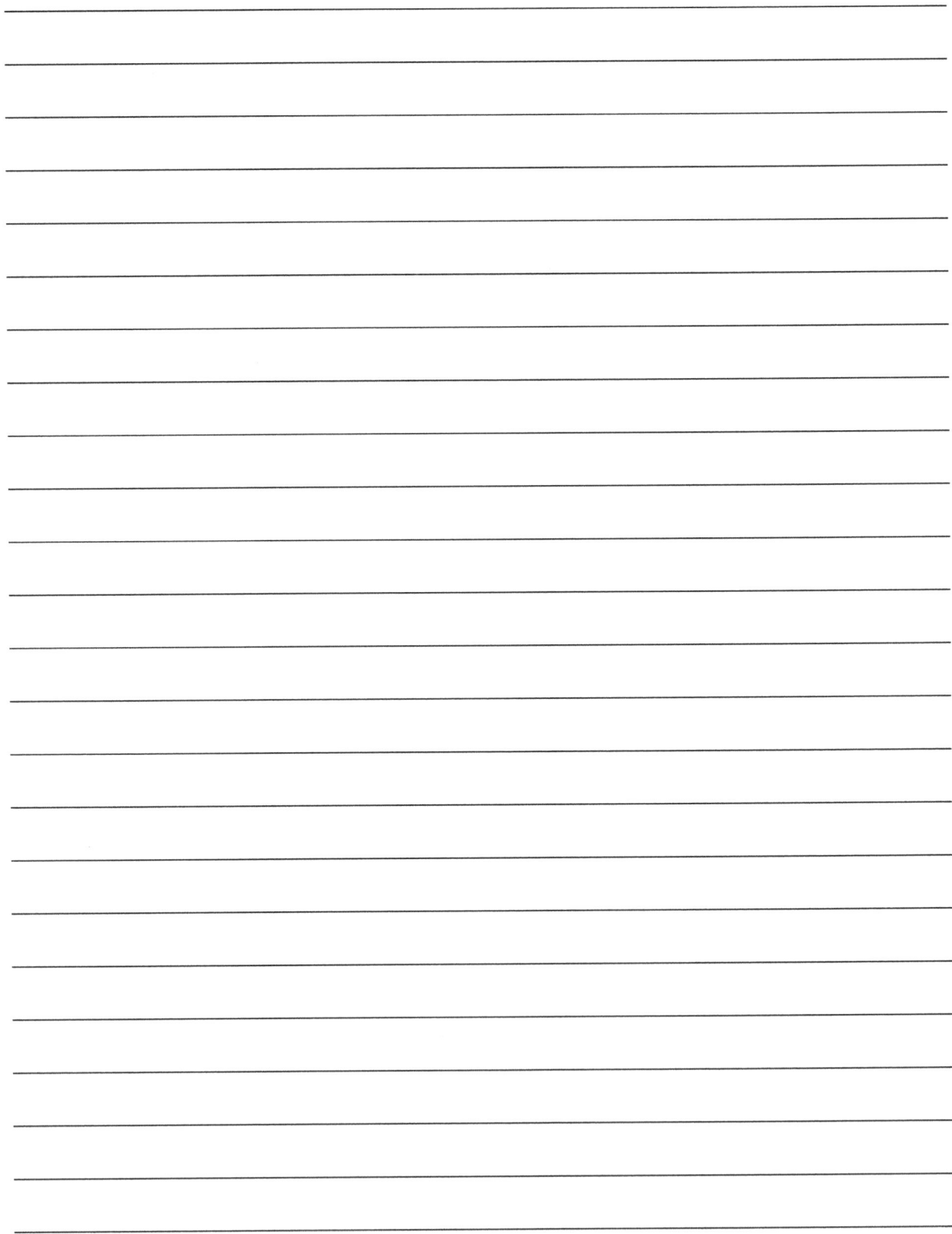

WORKSHEET 8

Name: z_____   Date:

a b c d e f g h i j k l m n o p q r s t u v w x y z

hiss miss shall cliff drill doll bill moss hull chess kill dress hill frizz gloss fluff shrill jazz stiff mess kiss less ass puff cross mill class stress snuff loss whizz shell gruff spell quell toss grill still glass off cuff spill overspill gull swell press express candy-floss buzz frill

☐ Cross out each letter of the alphabet in sequence

☐ Read aloud and colour each group of endings

☐ Find three more examples of each ending

ff	ll	ss	zz
puff	hill	glass	buzz

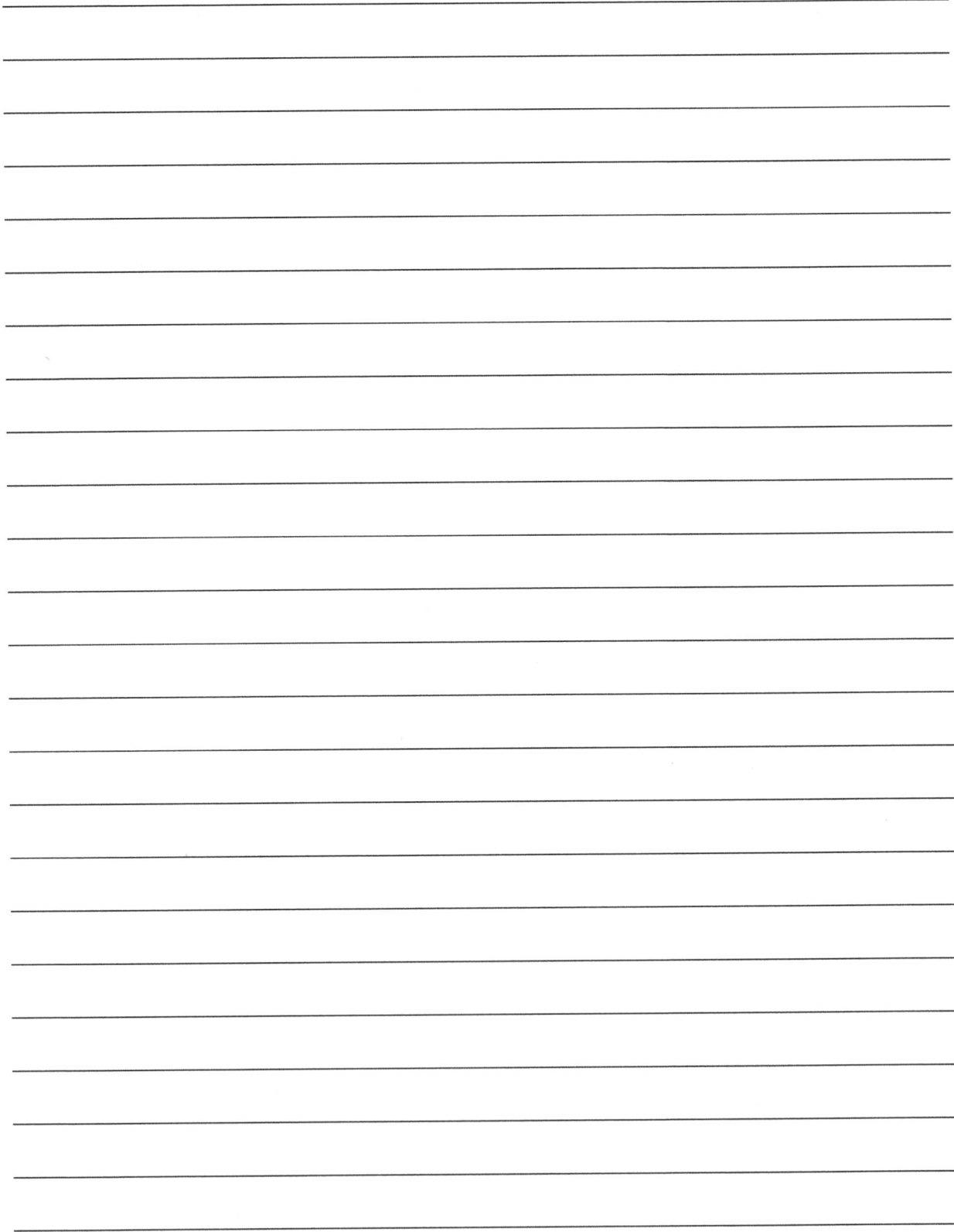

WORKSHEET 9

Name: _____ Date: _____

a b c d e f g h i j k l m n o p q r s t u v w x y z

born darn barn horn her corn surf bird burst first
term start firm smart cart port girl burn chart
curl dirt jerk sort perm lark harsh chirp stern
charm stir fern sport porch quirk spurt farm
birch church torn third sharp over slur lurch
worn exert churn yarn scarf zero

☐ Cross out each letter of the alphabet in sequence

☐ Read aloud and colour each group of sounds

☐ Find five examples of each sound

(ār)	(ôr)	(er) spelt er	(er) spelt ir	(er) spelt ur

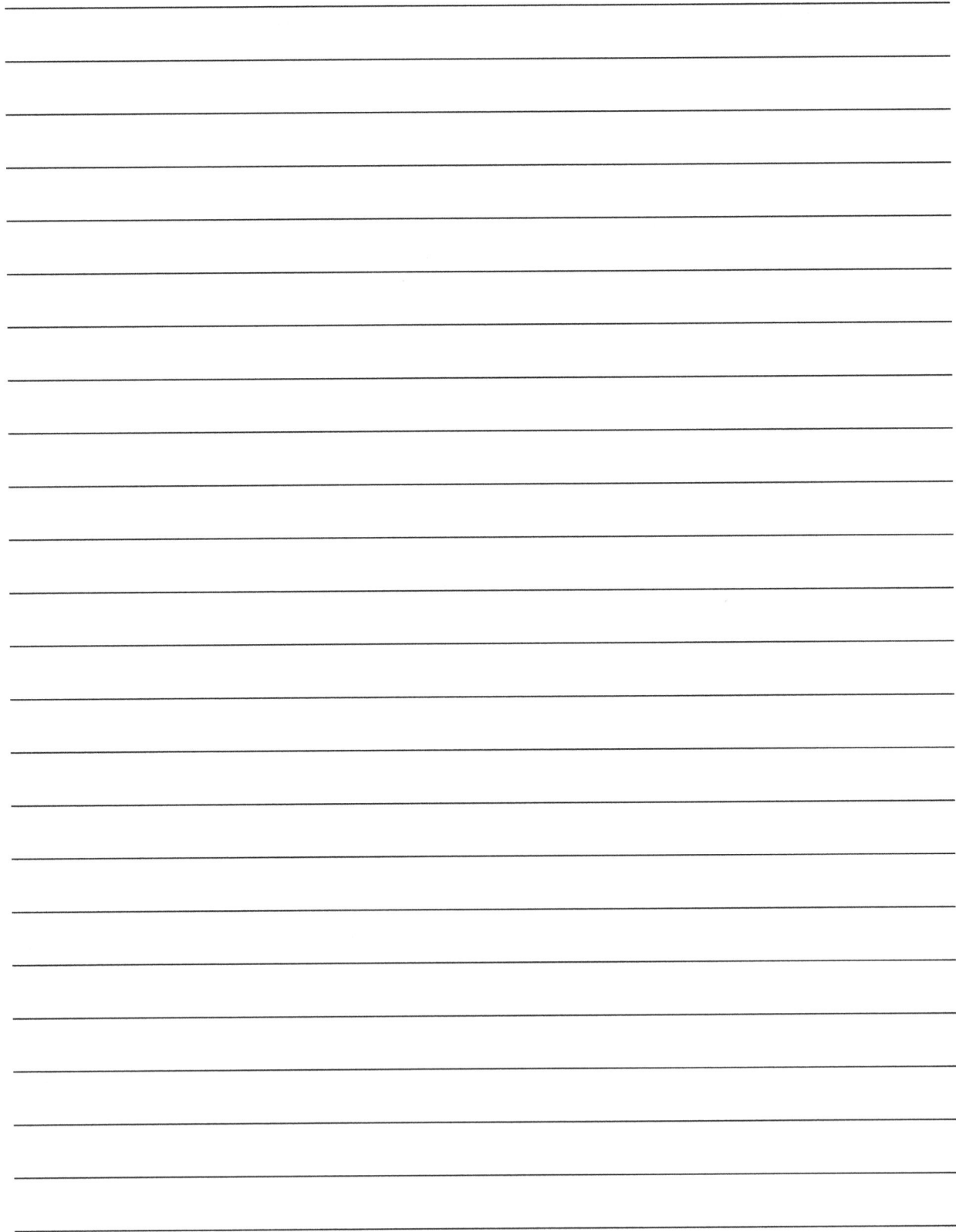

WORKSHEET 10

Name: _____ Date: _____

a b c d e f g h i j k l m n o p q r s t u v w x y z

hotpot wigwam goblin conduct oblong contest robin inland fabric sunset carpet garden confess humbug problem inject basket tartan antic splendid insect dentist magnet triplet piglet optic nutmeg quintet selfish brandish lemon metric rustic silver tablet tactic tractor bitter cobweb contact bandit combat convict hatbox picnic helmet lily victim admit zigzag

☐ Cross out each letter of the alphabet in sequence

☐ Read the words aloud

☐ Divide each word into two closed syllables

hot/pot	wig/wam	gob/lin	con/duct
oblong	fabric	sunset	brandish
dentist	triplet	picnic	contest
nutmeg	tactic	convict	cobweb

WORKSHEET 11

Name: _____ Date: _____

a b c d e f g h i j k l m n o p q r s t u v w x y z

cannot butter dagger copper button better dinner
fellow chatter batter adding shatter flatten mitten
judder fitting kipper carrot blotter batting rubber
matter cotton horrid adder inner potter robber lesson
quitter supper digger tennis ribbon upper stagger
flatter letter villa otter summer wedding pepper
hammer suffix yellow pillow slipper winner zipper

☐ Cross out each letter of the alphabet in sequence

☐ Read the words aloud

☐ Divide each word into two closed syllables

can/not	but/ton	dag/ger	cop/per
letter	dinner	ribbon	summer
tennis	kipper	yellow	lesson
wedding	matter	pepper	carrot

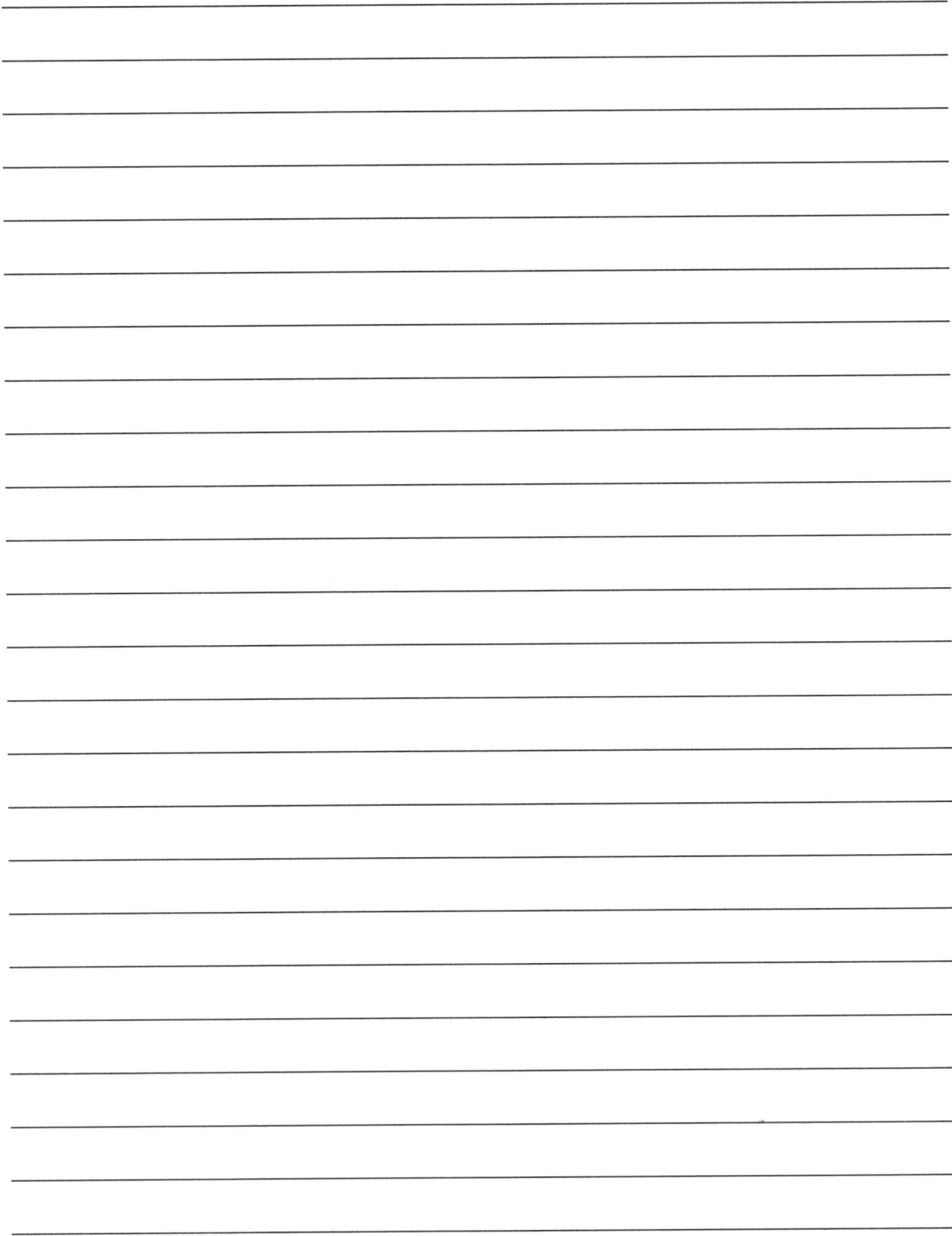

WORKSHEET 12

Name: _____ Date: _____

a b c d e f g h i j k l m n o p q r s t u v w x y z

date side cube tune late cake bake tide safe gale
flute hole five take fate joke bone dive lane mistake
slope like wine lake compete mine quote shake tube
strike hope dispute rake compute tame these vine
time complete wake quake ride pale explode gaze
wife yoke concrete save froze

☐ Cross out each letter of the alphabet in sequence

☐ Read aloud and colour each group of silent e words

☐ Find three more examples of each long vowel

(ā)	(ē)	(ī)	(ō)	(ū)
lake	compete	ride	slope	tune

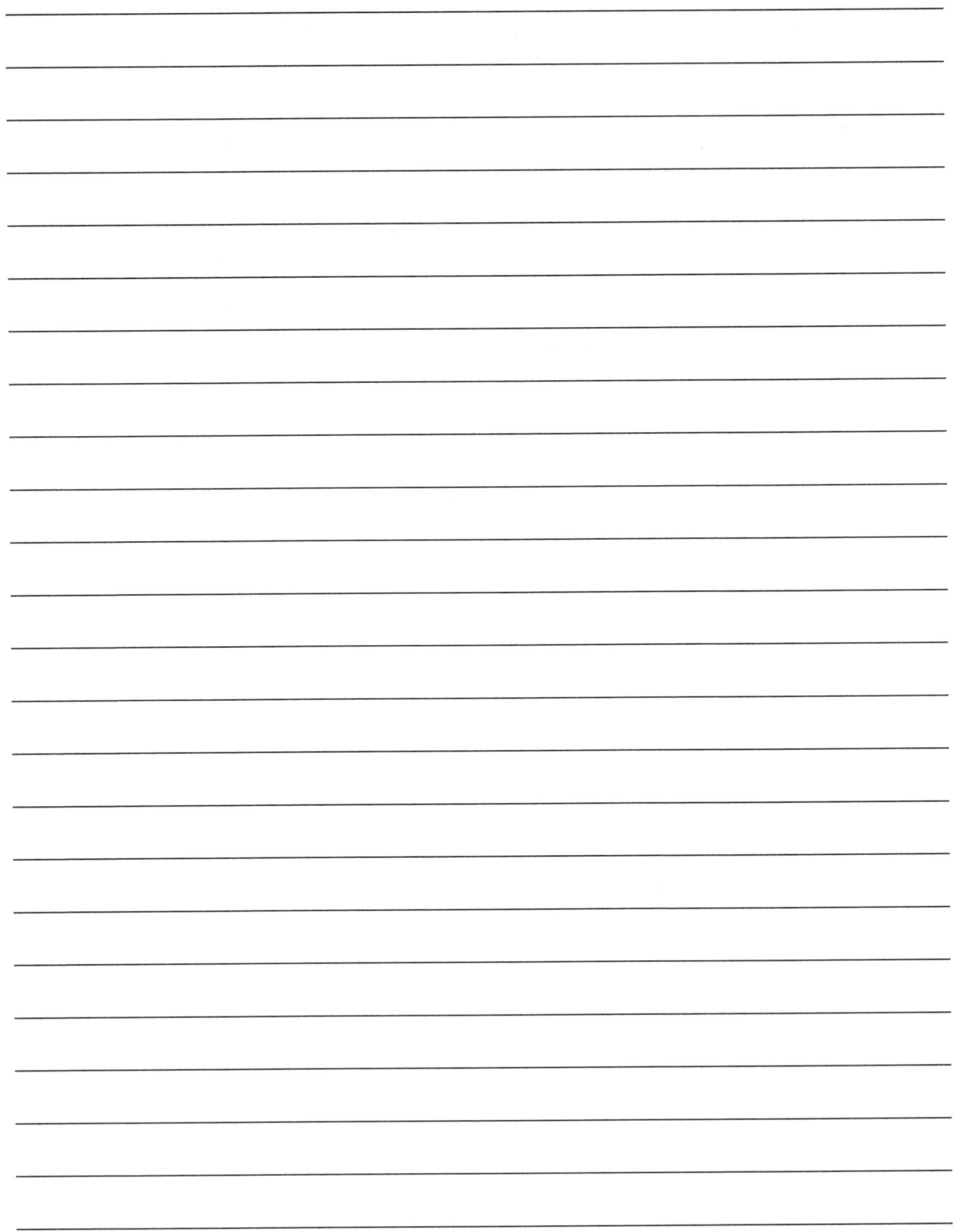

WORKSHEET 13

Name: _____   Date: _____

a b c d e f g h i j k l m n o p q r s t u v w x y z

bee aloof deep book feed cook been mood hook
goose feet cheese see agree choose foolish food
jeep freedom green look moon school afternoon
smooth breeze screech knee proof keep tooth good
shook squeeze spoon teeth rook seventeen free
room cuckoo sleeve sweet took exceed queen
freeze sleepy wood zoom

☐ Cross out each letter of the alphabet in sequence

☐ Read aloud and colour each group of sounds

☐ Find three more examples for each column

($\bar{ee}$)	($\bar{oo}$)	($\breve{oo}$)
deep	food	good

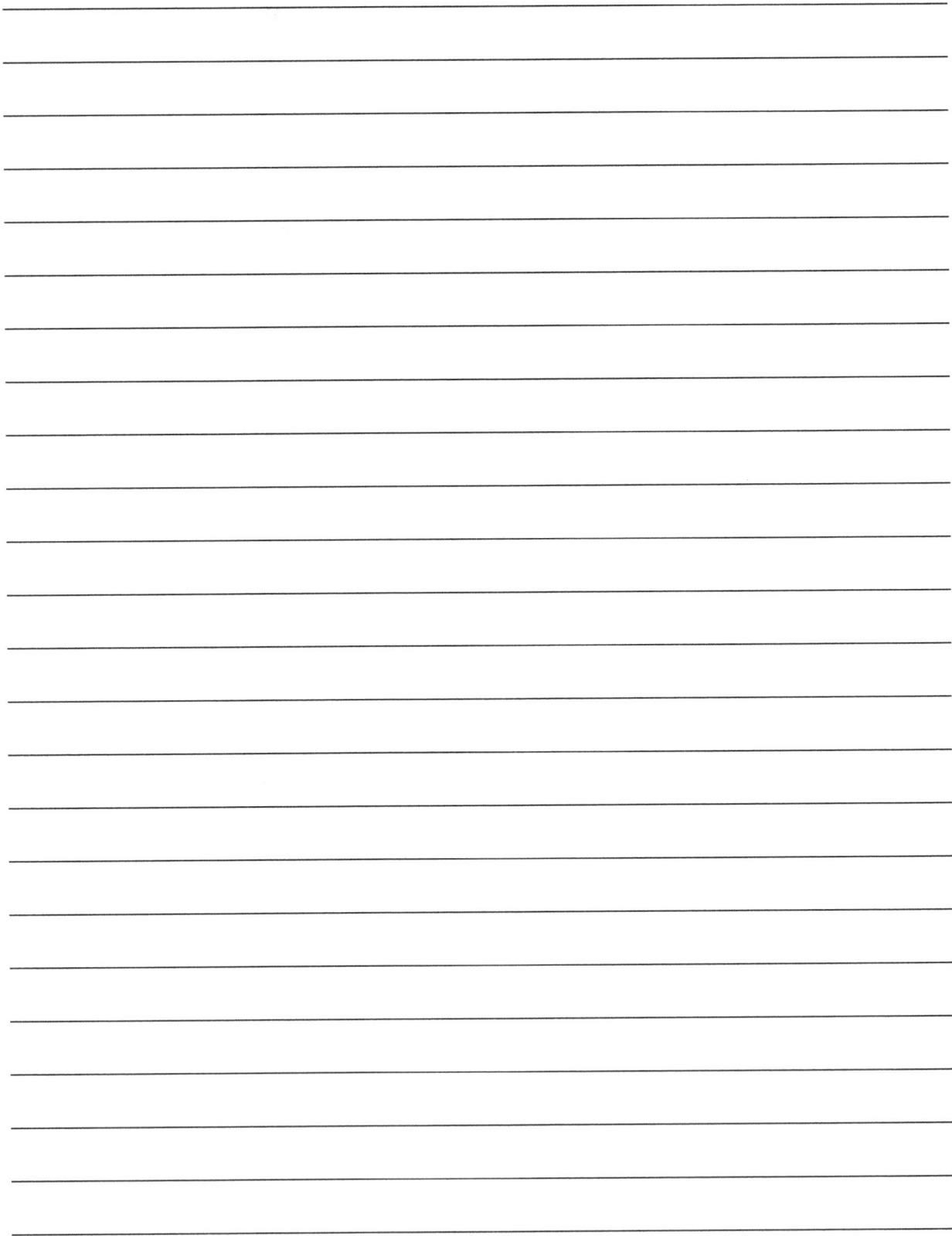

WORKSHEET 14

Name: _____   Date: _____

a b c d e f g h i j k l m n o p q r s t u v w x y z

rock panic back drink lock cabin check Atlantic attack frantic bank magic corner hectic junk fantastic static clinic tank pocket camera cactus elastic calendar silk locket kennel pink quick Pacific rink septic bucket sock havoc folk ketchup wicket canal keen milk toxic brick sink yolk kitten wink trunk colonize plastic

☐ Cross out each letter of the alphabet in sequence

☐ Read aloud and colour each group of words

☐ Find three more examples for each column

c-	k-	-c	-ck	-k
cactus	kennel	magic	check	drink

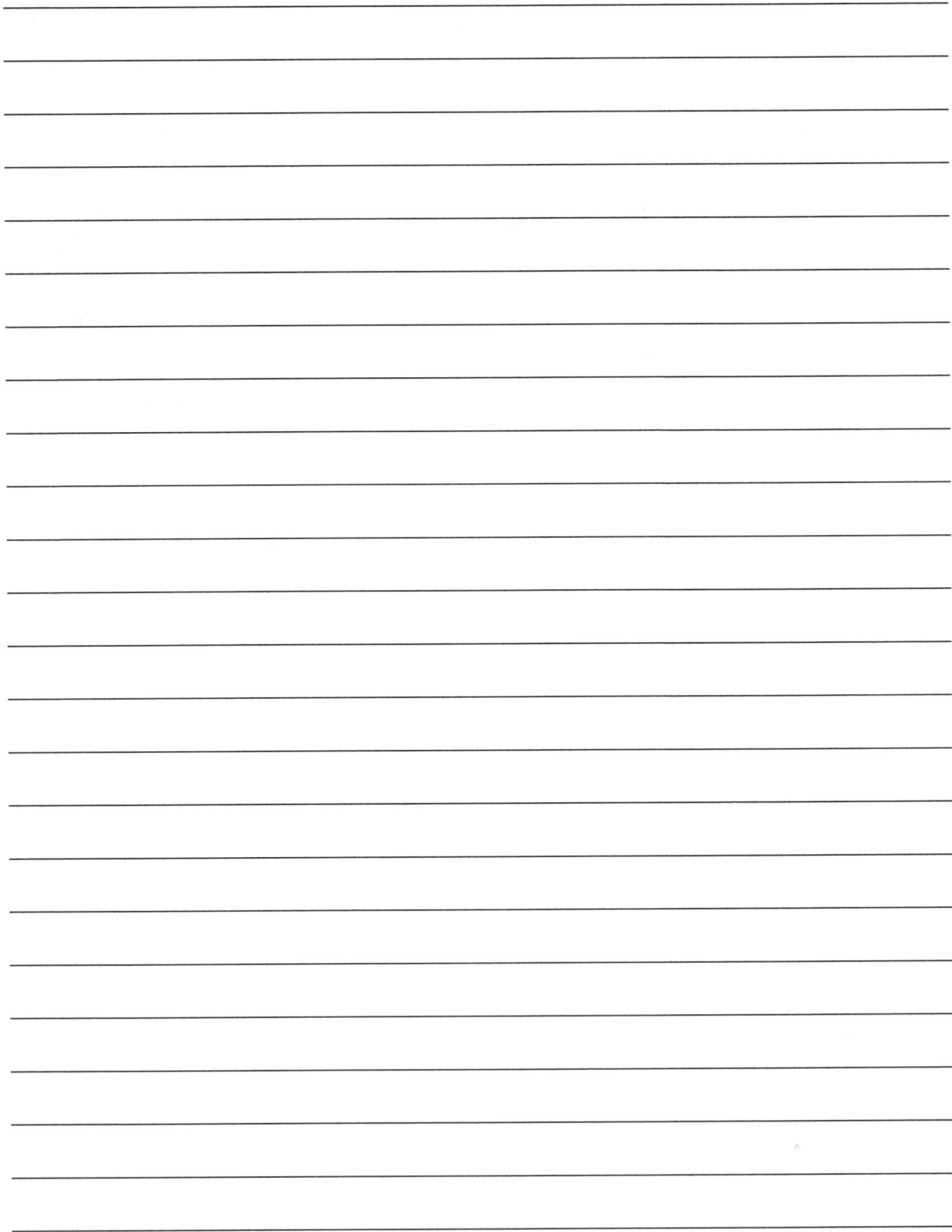

WORKSHEET 15

Name: _____   Date: _____

a b c d e f g h i j k l m n o p q r s t u v w x y z

price ace loose boss nice dose fleece place absence grace ice spice house practice justice police France kindliness prince chase office rice mass lace lease lice notice piece moose since acquaintance peace trace distress reduce across release advice happiness practise difference twice existence fuss service abyss sentence confuse laziness address

☐ Cross out each letter of the alphabet in sequence

☐ Read aloud and colour group of sounds

☐ Write four words in each column

-ce	-se	-ss

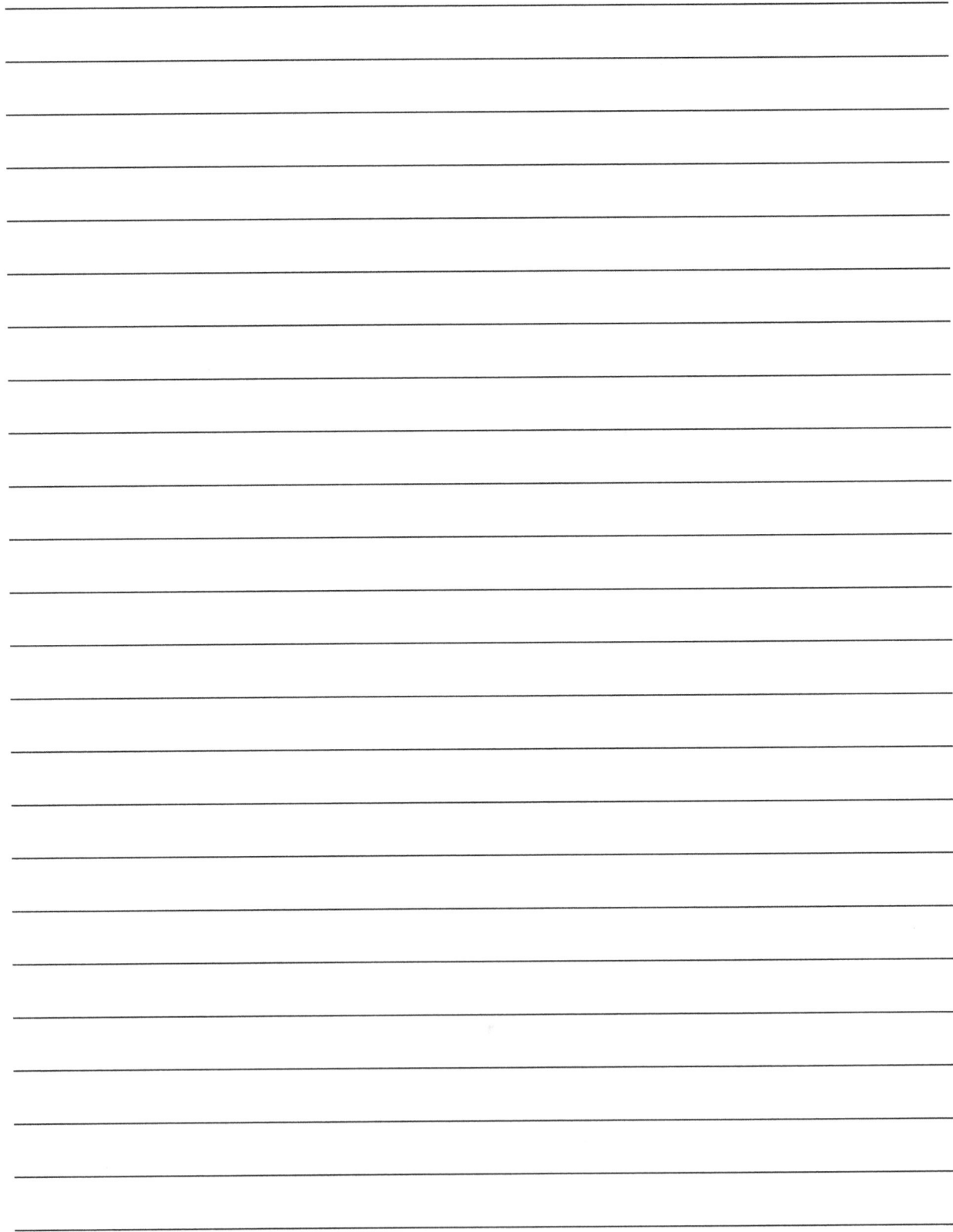

WORKSHEET 16

Name: _____   Date: _____

a b c d e f g h i j k l m n o p q r s t u v w x y z

battle cuddle table idle trifle giggle rifle castle thistle duffle fiddle hurdle cradle shingle bubble poodle ladle hobble simple jumble kettle smuggle rattle bristle angle gobble muddle paddle saddle quibble apple eagle needle noble rustle snuffle title single pebble invisible purple dwindle triangle example puzzle wrestle meddle yaffle whistle dazzle

☐ Cross out each letter of the alphabet in sequence

☐ Read aloud and colour each group of words

☐ Write two examples of each stable final syllable

-ble	-dle	-fle	-gle

-ple	-stle	-tle	-zle

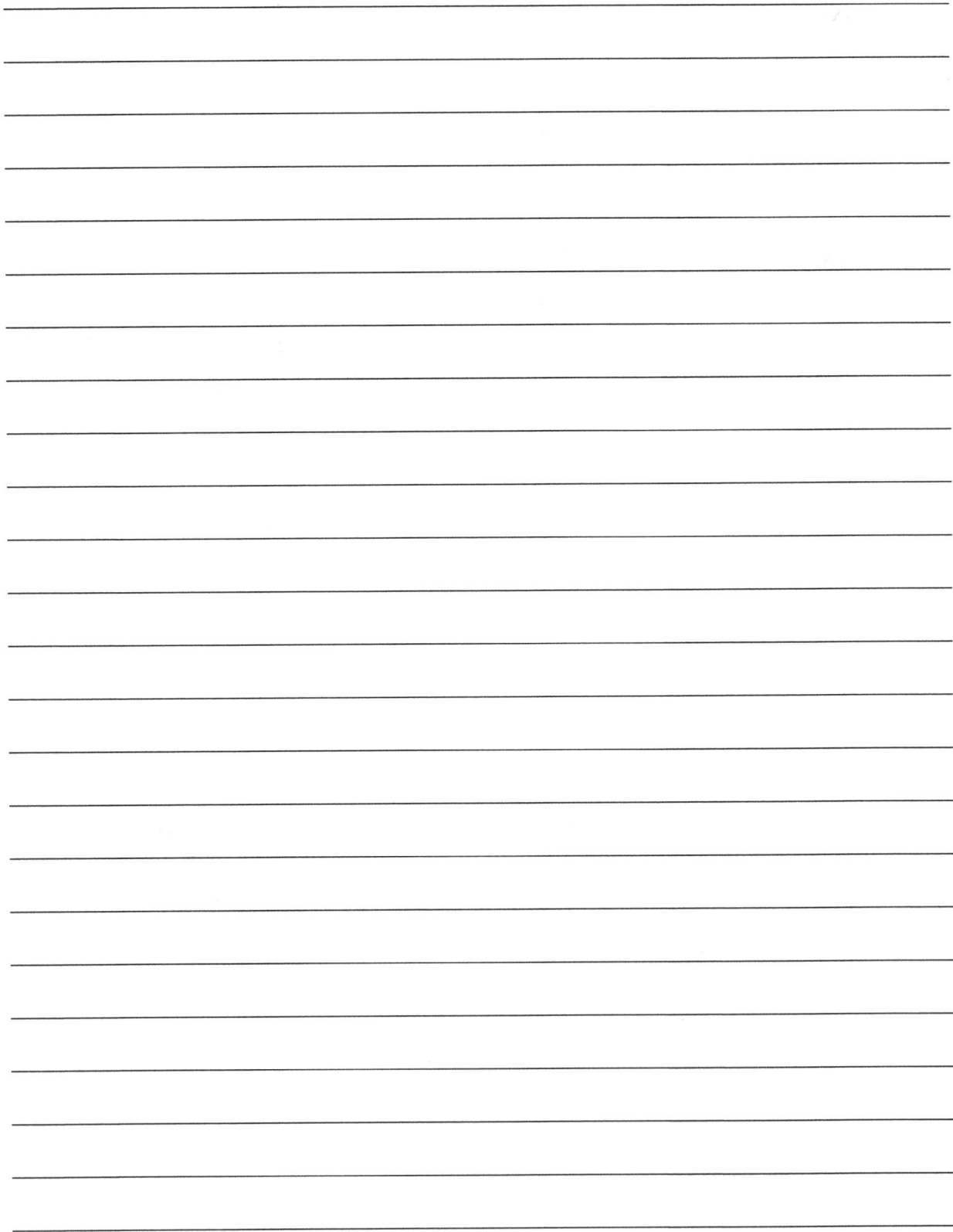

WORKSHEET 17

Name: _____ Date: _____

a b c d e f g h i j k l m n o p q r s t u v w x y z

tackle barnacle ankle twinkle radical article freckle
political crinkle magical chuckle cuticle juridical
speckle musical tickle chronicle trickle spectacle
pickle tropical quizzical nautical pinnacle crackle
tentacle obstacle oracle prickle cackle heckle buckle
identical topical sprinkle physical particle vehicle
cubicle sparkle winkle electrical practical
extraphysical classical technical manacle wrinkle
zoological bicycle

☐ Cross out each letter of the alphabet in sequence

☐ Read aloud and colour each group of words

☐ Write five words in each column below

-cal	-ckle	-cle	-kle

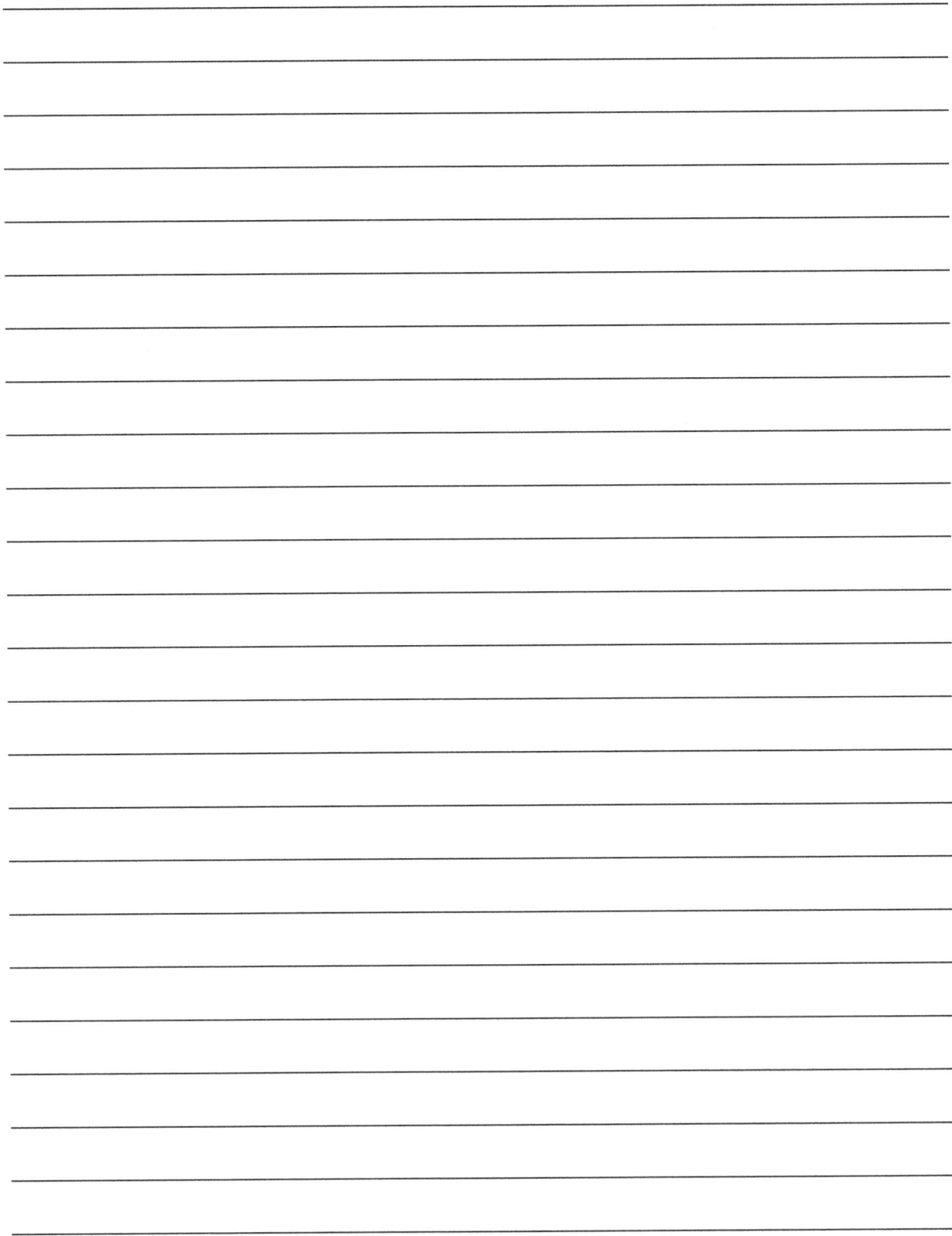

WORKSHEET 18

Name: _____   Date: _____

a b c d e f g h i j k l m n o p q r s t u v w x y z

rain brain stay nail chain betray drain remain
birthday afraid grain say tail holiday today jail again
raise stray haystack against snail pain entertain
midday decay castaway Spain stowaway waist
plaice obtain quail delay trail dismay complain train
unafraid yesterday contain vain display wait explain
faint portrait spray maize motorway

☐ Cross out each letter of the alphabet in sequence

☐ Read aloud and colour the two groups of words

☐ Write five words in each column

ai	ay

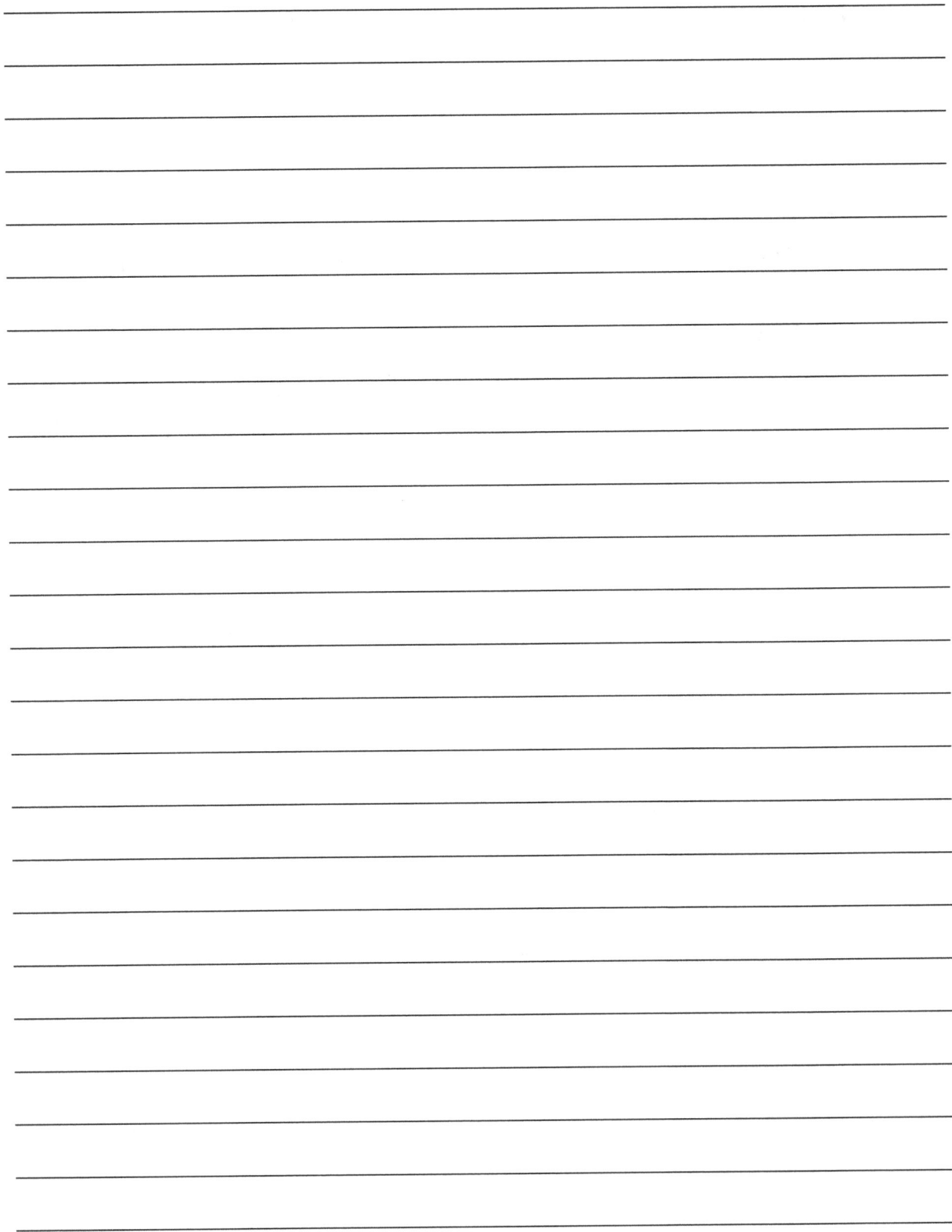

WORKSHEET 19

Name: _____ Date: _____

a b c d e f g h i j k l m n o p q r s t u v w x y z

road crow elbow allow cloud brown bellow bowl aloud follow goal about clown shallow growl groan mountain tower jowl goat know shower found owl mouse throat throw around trousers power float moat aquashow frown thousand glow trout scarecrow vow discount roast coax scowl county grow town ounce outsize hoax mouth

☐ Cross out each letter of the alphabet in sequence

☐ Read aloud and colour the four groups of words

☐ Find four more examples for each column

(ō)	(ō)	(ou)	(ou)
goat	grow	found	brown

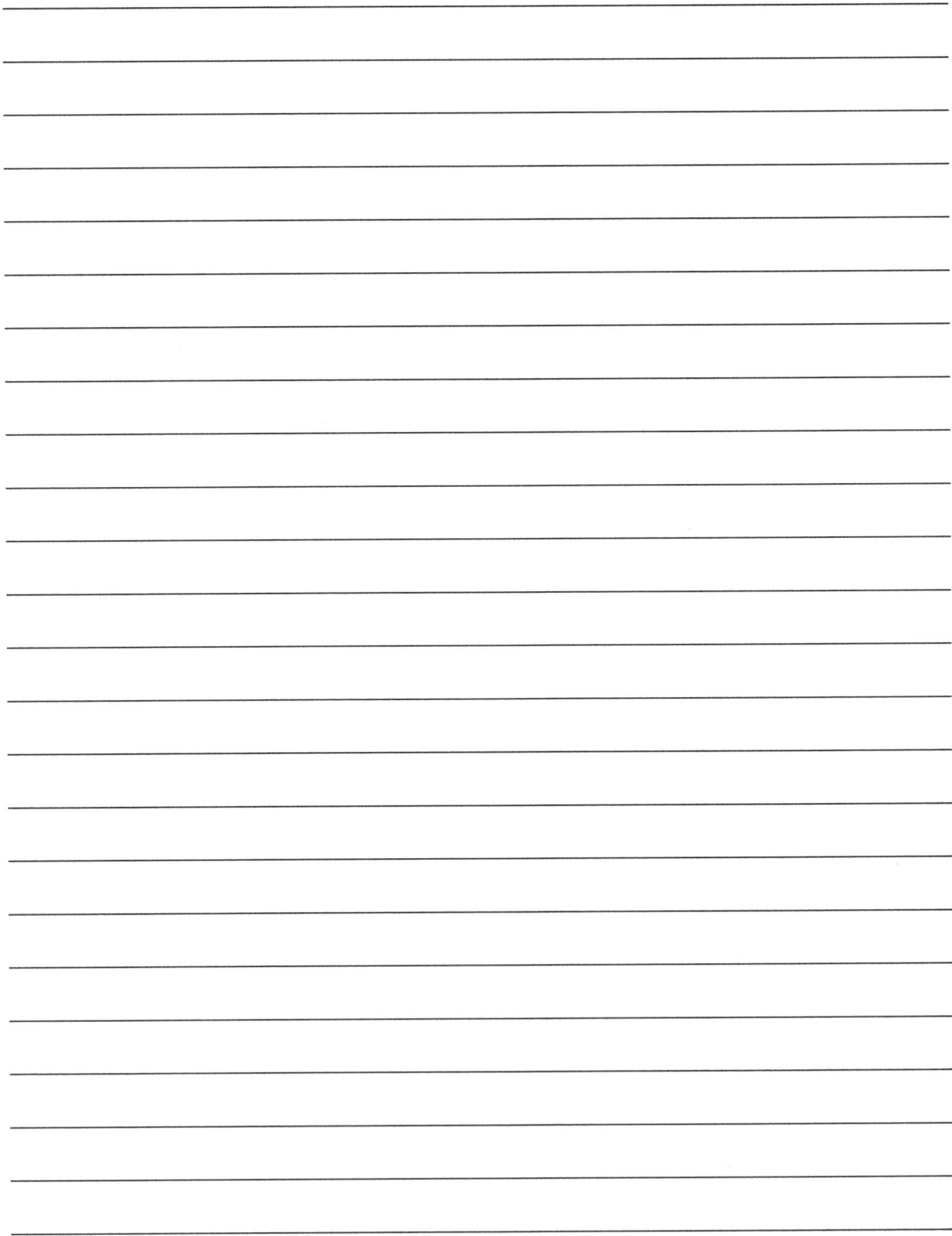

WORKSHEET 20

Name: _____   Date: _____

a b c d e f g h i j k l m n o p q r s t u v w x y z

mean bread stream steady each health tread break
flea beach crease breath breathe great cheat
creature please breakage instead greatly jealousy
pleasure grease breakdown pleasant deaf scream
thread pheasant feather colleague stealth peach
disease squeak speak treasure dream treachery
dreadful spread teacher steak reveal reason wealth
Greatorex yeast heaven zealous

☐ Cross out each letter of the alphabet in sequence

☐ Read aloud and colour the three groups of words

☐ Find three more examples for each column

(ē)	(ĕ)	(ā)
stream	heaven	break

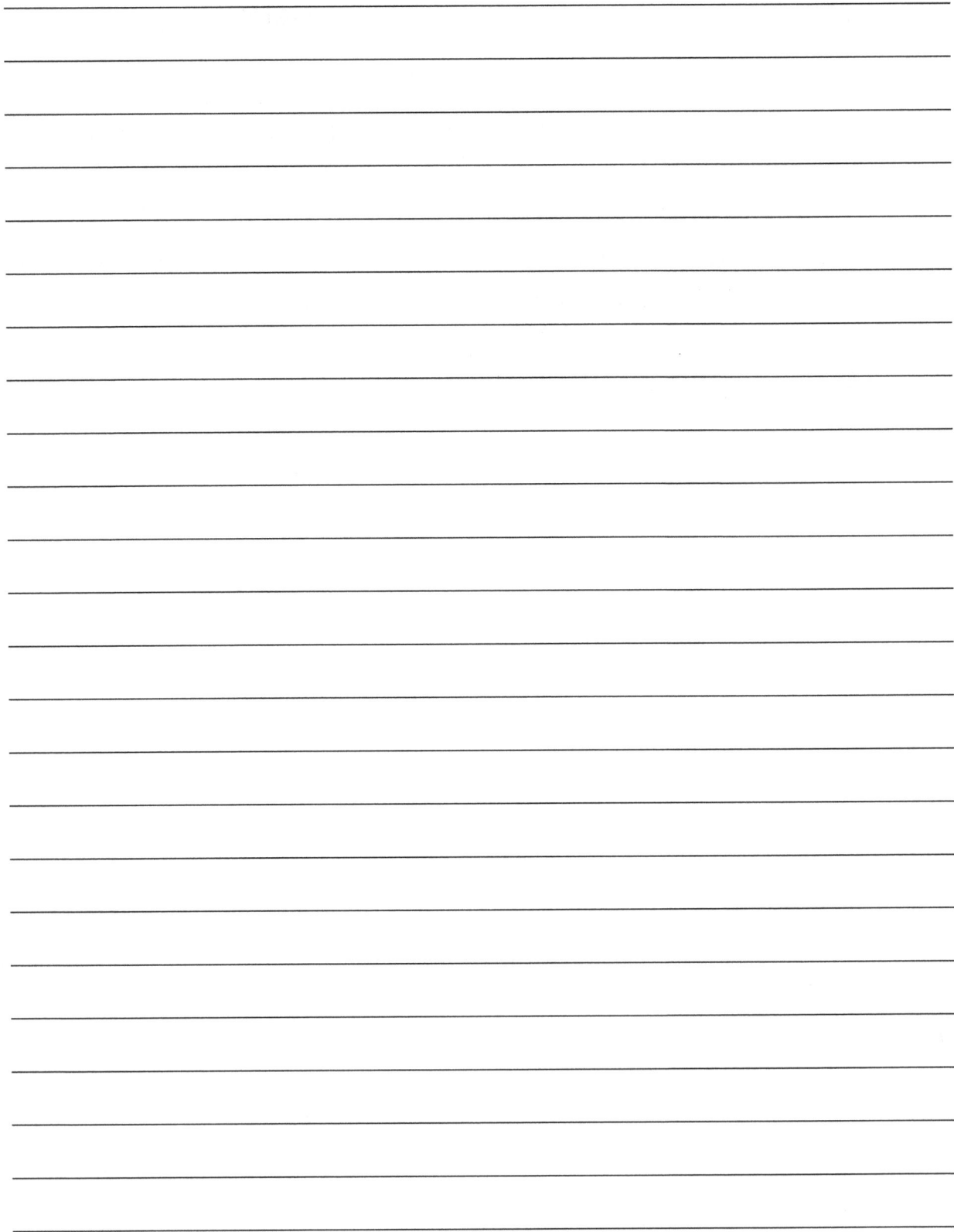

WORKSHEET 21

Name: _____ Date: _____

a b c d e f g h i j k l m n o p q r s t u v w x y z

draw bawl raw crawl dawn sauce caution awful daunted bauble gnaw saucer haunted caustic fault applause jaunty hawk August haulier haunt cause traumatic pause lawn raucous haulage launch squaw pawn squawk pauper saunter claw jigsaw laundry dawdle straw hawthorn law vault taunt jaw exhausted awkward awning tawdry astronaut gauze audience

☐ Cross out each letter of the alphabet in sequence

☐ Read aloud and colour the two groups of words

☐ Find five words for each column

au	aw

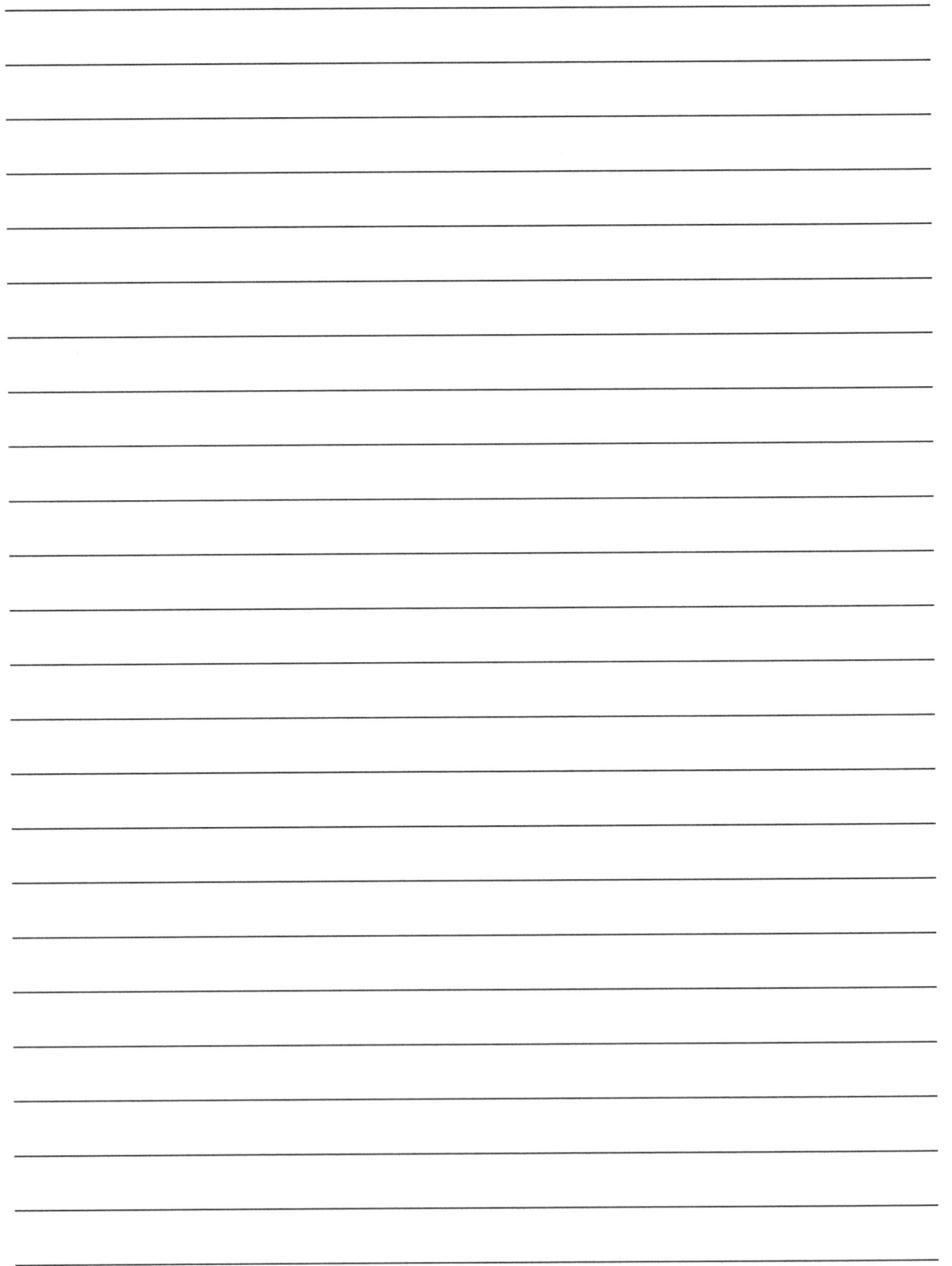

WORKSHEET 22

Name: _____ Date: _____

a b c d e f g h i j k l m n o p q r s t u v w x y z

new argue dew due blew few deuce blue drew feud chew clue glue flew threw stew mildew Europe jewel grew eureka sleuth pharmaceutical pneumonia subdue pew statue true knew queue eucalyptus curlew newt avenue shrewd renew neurotic corkscrew neurology value rheumatism neutral crew tissue barbecue eutaxia therapeutic yew continue Zeus

☐ Cross out each letter of the alphabet in sequence

☐ Read aloud and colour the three groups of words

☐ Find five words for each column

eu	ew	ue

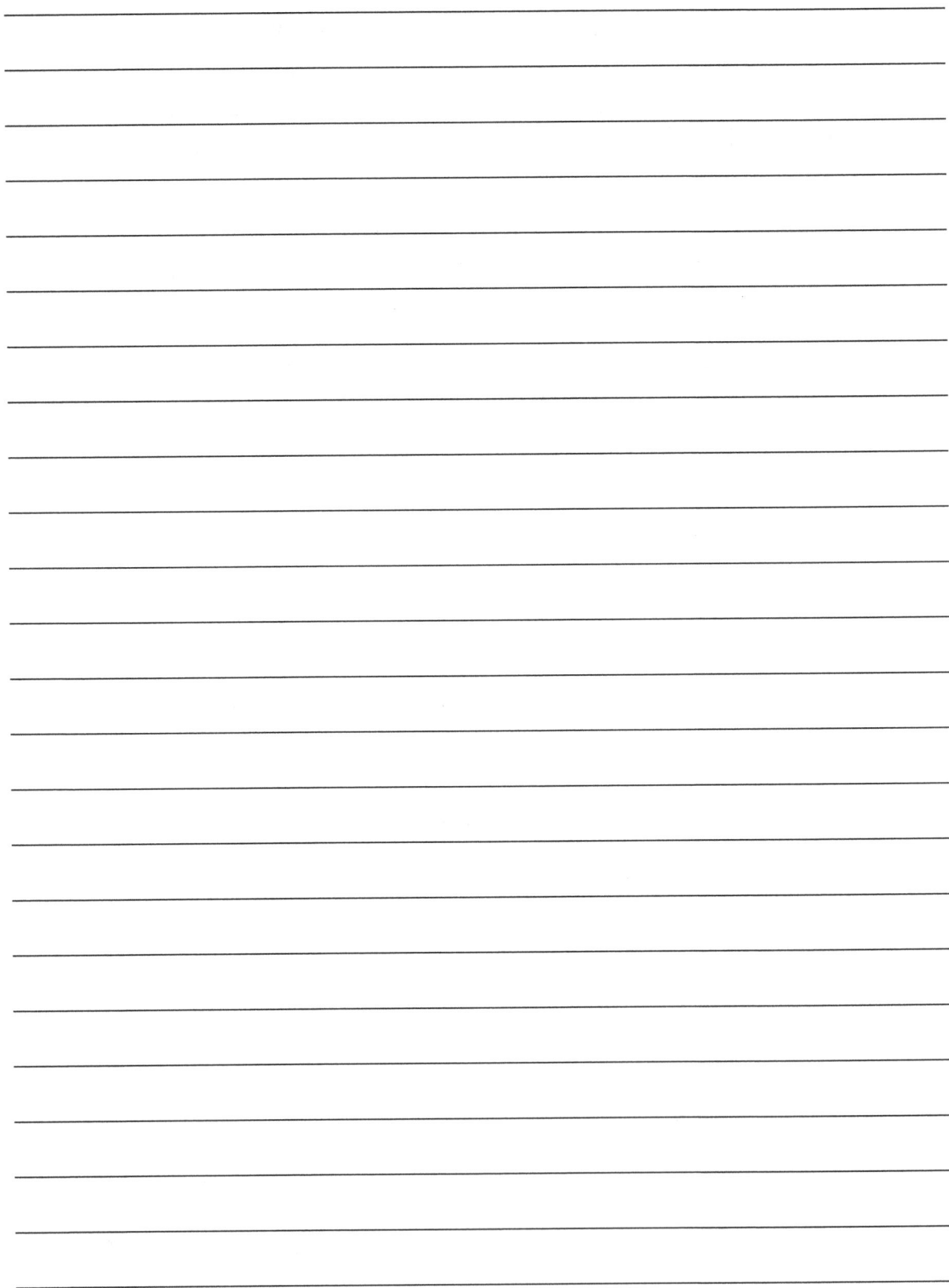

WORKSHEET 23

Name: _____ Date: _____

a b c d e f g h i j k l m n o p q r s t u v w x y z

large gentle badge giant gem lodge cage giraffe hedge fudge July huge just edge dodge subject January genius rage luggage sage general joking ridge ledge object smudge jury ginger grudge barge geography jonquil German injection plunge gymnastics drudge bridge adjective judge page wage juxtapose June wedge jubilant joyful hinge generalization

☐ Cross out each letter of the alphabet in sequence

☐ Read aloud and colour the four groups of words

☐ Find four words to write in each column

j-	g-	-dge	-ge

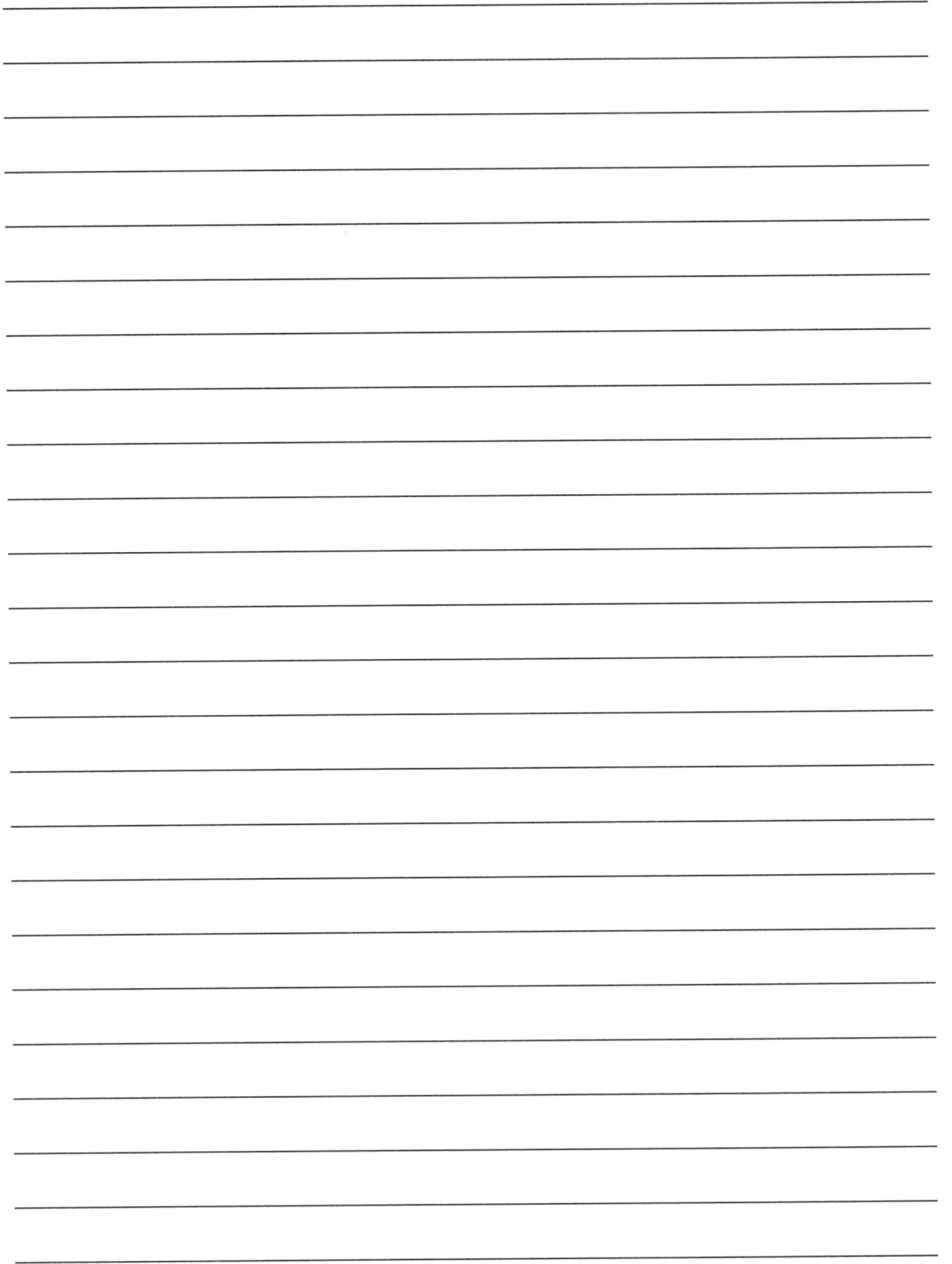

WORKSHEET 24

Name: _____   Date: _____

a b c d e f g h i j k l m n o p q r s t u v w x y z

telephone fatigue February coffee dolphin alphabet fierce physics autograph traffic Joseph radiography fickle farther catastrophe photograph emphasis buffalo failure phantom fanatic physique philosophy autobiography photocopy sphere prophet daffodil suffer telegraph favourite profit paragraph orphan different curfew apostrophe triumph fixture offer toffee photography sulphur furious phenomenal pharmacist fizz pharmacy factory faithfully

- ☐ Cross out each letter of the alphabet in sequence
- ☐ Read aloud and colour the three groups of words
- ☐ Join all the words to their meanings

apostrophe	exhaustion
autobiography	one who prepares medicines
catastrophe	sign (') for a missing letter
fatigue	exceptional, extraordinary
phenomenal	disastrous occurrence
pharmacist	person's self-written life story

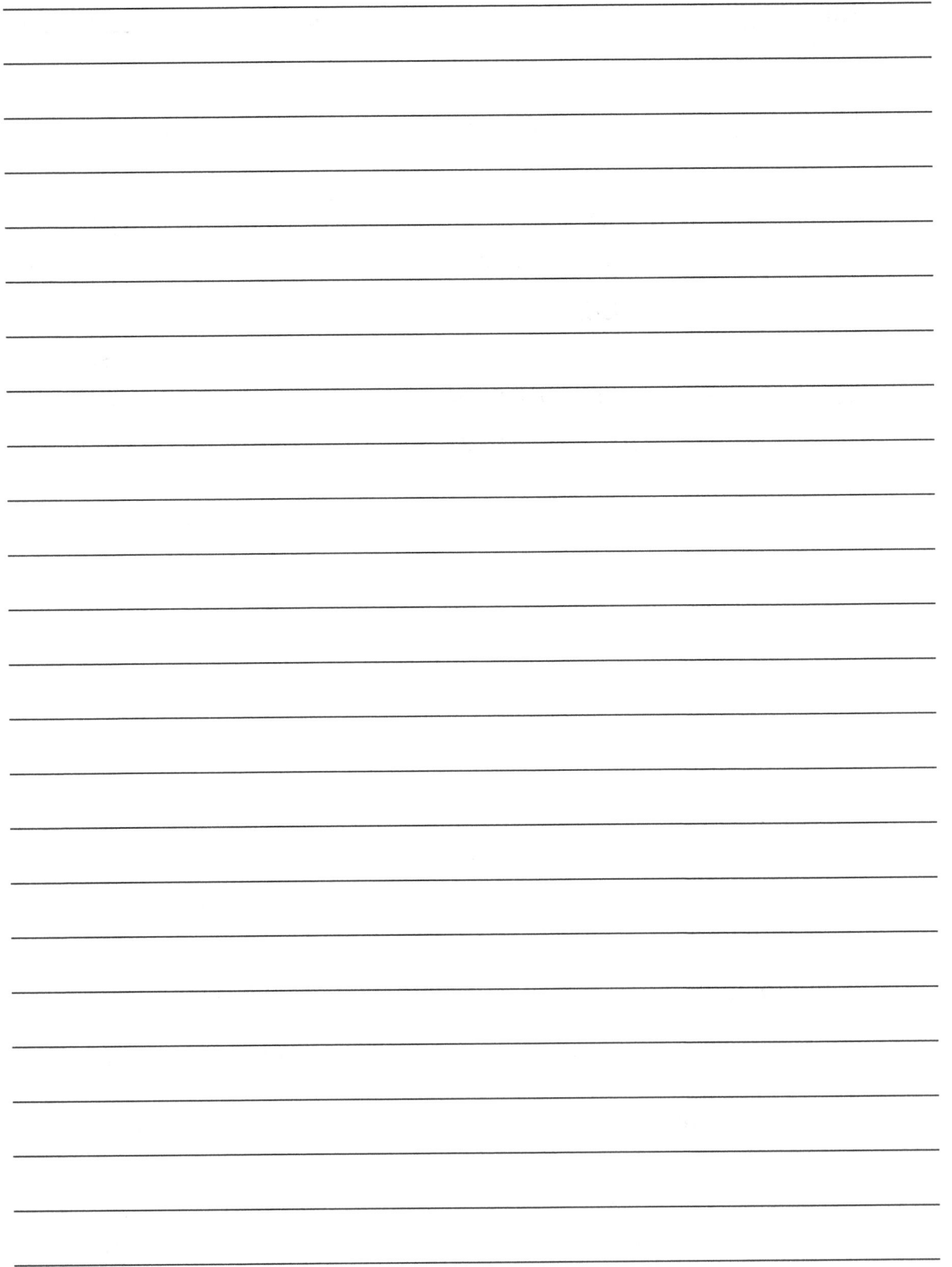

WORKSHEET 25

Name: _____ Date: _____

a b c d e f g h i j k l m n o p q r s t u v w x y z

dangerous   bonus   glorious   focus   humorous
generous tremendous courageous fabulous circus
delicious   conscious   gracious   perilous   famous
thunderous ruinous jealous numerous enormous
cantankerous fictitious virus luxurious serious
terminus mysterious fungus suspicious crocus
querulous mountainous nervous ambitious precious
status wondrous marvellous monotonous poisonous
anxious contagious census tedious obvious cautious
victorious joyous spacious hazardous

☐ Cross out each letter of the alphabet in sequence

☐ Read aloud and colour the three groups of words

☐ Join the words below to their meanings

anxious	imaginary
crocus	many
enormous	amusing, funny'
fictitious	plant with a corm
humorous	worried
numerous	huge

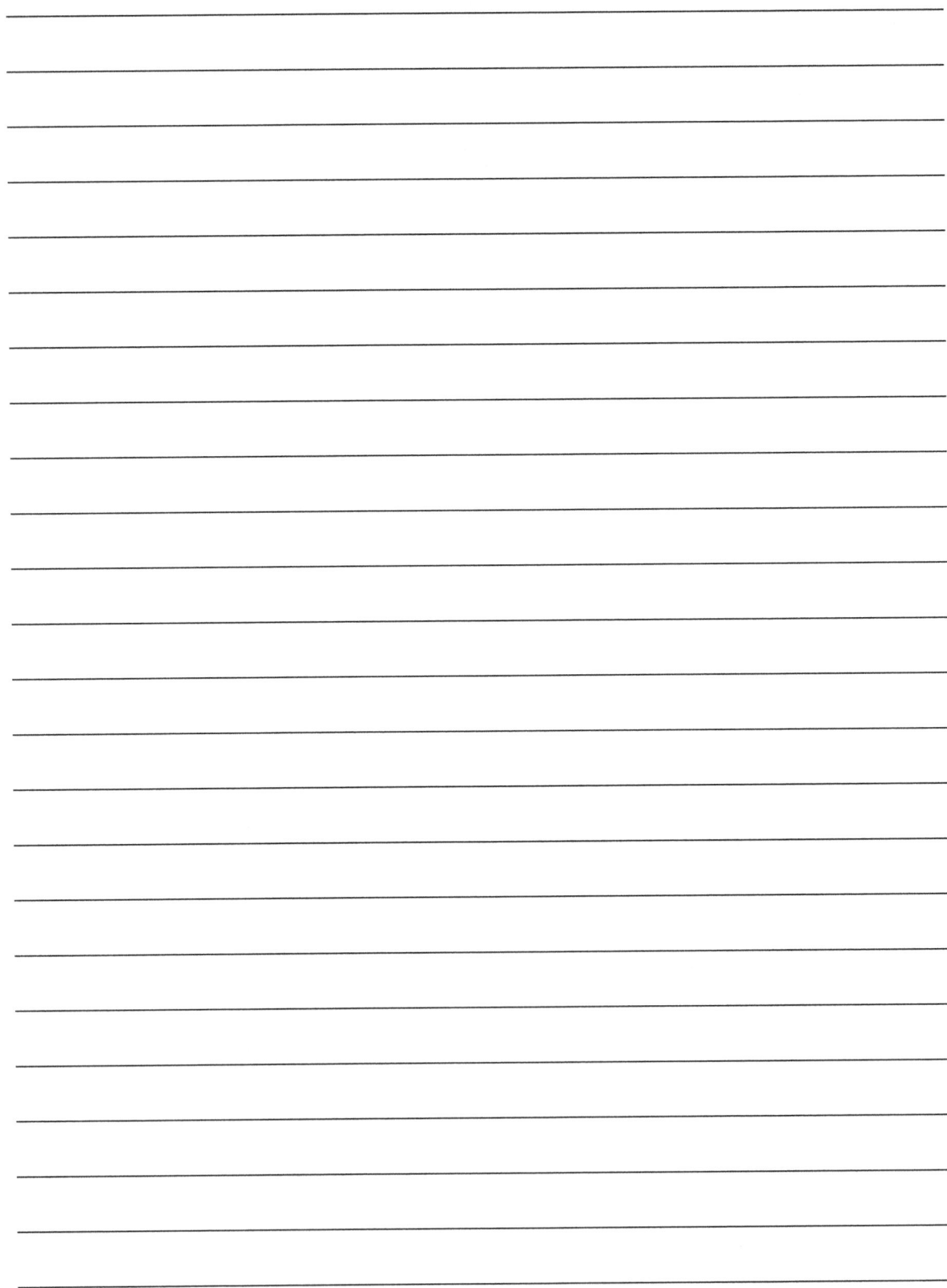

WORKSHEET 26

Name: _____   Date:

a b c d e f g h i j k l m n o p q r s t u v w x y z

distraction submersion permission population vacation diversion profession ignition motion comprehension juxtaposition aggression technician embarkation completion recognition imposition dictation electrician superstition lotion inquisition condition politician compulsion inspection immersion nation impression magician propulsion optician depression taxation session innovation situation tuition musician beautician workstation discussion attention fixation aggravation gyration examination expression procession realization

☐ Cross out each letter of the alphabet in sequence

☐ Read aloud and colour the four groups of words

☐ Choose a suitable word for each of the following

holiday =

prestidigitator =

teaching =

understanding =

another route =

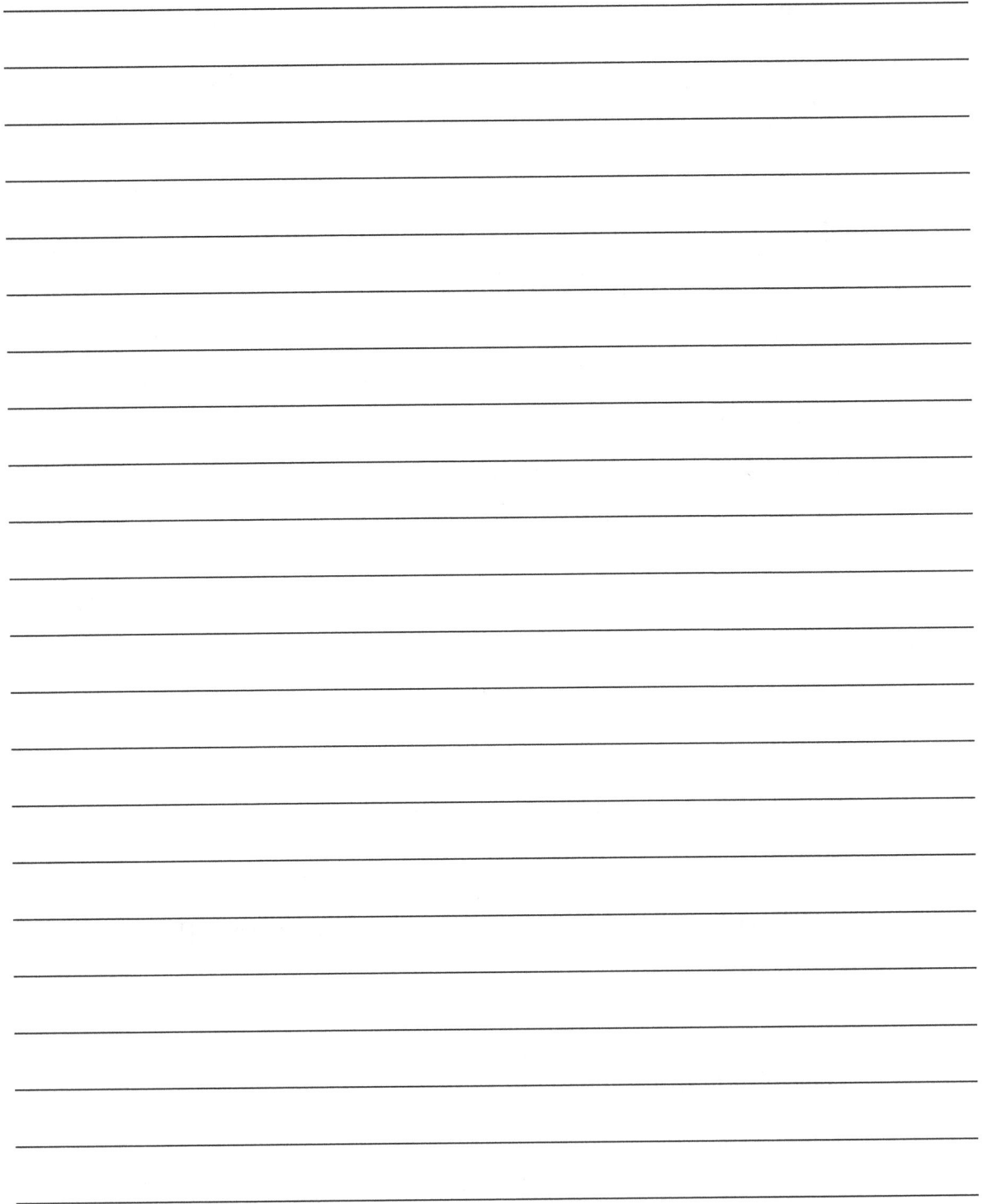

WORKSHEET 27

Name: _____ Date: _____

a b c d e f g h i j k l m n o p q r s t u v w x y z

beginning ache enough business already colour answer doctor special cough fascinate believe government immediately rhyme foreign guess grammar jewellery knowledge weather whether rhythm necessary right write people mystery successful quiet minute separate quite sincerely niece pigeon exaggerate judgement meant eventually course cushion parliament nephew apparatus exhibition library receive temperature zoology

☐ Cross out each letter of the alphabet in sequence

☐ Read the words

☐ Join each word to its correct description

quiet	brother or sister's daughter
quite	measured beat
nephew	completely or rather
niece	word endings sound the same
rhyme	brother or sister's son
rhythm	absence of noise

Word Lists

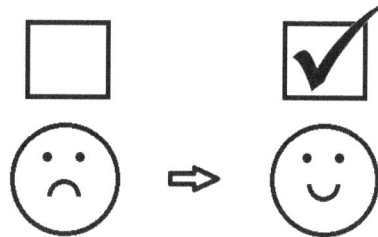

WORD LIST 1

1	bed	☐	26	log	☐
2	big	☐	27	man	☐
3	bin	☐	28	mop	☐
4	bit	☐	29	mug	☐
	box	☐	30	net	☐
6	bun	☐	31	not	☐
7	bus	☐	32	pen	☐
8	but	☐	33	pet	☐
9	can	☐	34	pin	☐
10	cat	☐	35	quit	☐
11	cot	☐	36	red	☐
12	cup	☐	37	rug	☐
13	dog	☐	38	run	☐
14	fat	☐	39	sit	☐
15	fox	☐	40	sun	☐
16	fun	☐	41	ten	☐
17	hat	☐	42	tin	☐
18	hen	☐	43	top	☐
19	hit	☐	44	van	☐
20	hop	☐	45	vet	☐
21	hug	☐	46	wet	☐
22	hut	☐	47	win	☐
23	jam	☐	48	yes	☐
24	kit	☐	49	yet	☐
25	leg	☐	50	zip	☐

WORD LIST 2

1	act	☐	26	kept	☐
2	and	☐	27	kilt	☐
3	belt	☐	28	lamp	☐
4	bold	☐	29	land	☐
5	calf	☐	30	lift	☐
6	camp	☐	31	lost	☐
7	cost	☐	32	melt	☐
8	dust	☐	33	must	☐
9	elf	☐	34	nest	☐
10	elm	☐	35	pond	☐
11	end	☐	36	quilt	☐
12	exact	☐	37	raft	☐
13	fact	☐	38	sand	☐
14	felt	☐	39	soft	☐
15	film	☐	40	tact	☐
16	gasp	☐	41	tent	☐
17	gift	☐	42	test	☐
18	gold	☐	43	told	☐
19	golf	☐	44	vest	☐
20	hand	☐	45	went	☐
21	helm	☐	46	wept	☐
22	help	☐	47	west	☐
23	hint	☐	48	wind	☐
24	hold	☐	49	yelp	☐
25	jump	☐	50	zest	☐

WORD LIST 3

1	crab	☐	26	slit	☐
2	crag	☐	27	slot	☐
3	cram	☐	28	slug	☐
4	crazy	☐	29	smash	☐
5	crib	☐	30	smog	☐
6	crop	☐	31	smug	☐
7	crush	☐	32	smut	☐
8	crux	☐	33	span	☐
9	cry	☐	34	spend	☐
10	French	☐	35	spin	☐
11	fresh	☐	36	spit	☐
12	fret	☐	37	spot	☐
13	frog	☐	38	spun	☐
14	from	☐	39	tram	☐
15	frost	☐	40	trap	☐
16	jog-trot	☐	41	travel	☐
17	plan	☐	42	trick	☐
18	plaque	☐	43	trim	☐
19	plod	☐	44	trip	☐
20	plot	☐	45	trod	☐
21	plug	☐	46	trust	☐
22	plum	☐	47	twenty	☐
23	slid	☐	48	twig	☐
24	slim	☐	49	twin	☐
25	slip	☐	50	twist	☐

WORD LIST 4

1	blot	☐	26	glen	☐
2	clan	☐	27	glove	☐
3	clap	☐	28	glum	☐
4	clash	☐	29	glut	☐
5	clef	☐	30	grid	☐
6	clip	☐	31	grim	☐
7	clique	☐	32	grip	☐
8	clog	☐	33	grub	☐
9	clop	☐	34	jet-black	☐
10	clot	☐	35	pram	☐
11	drab	☐	36	prim	☐
12	drank	☐	37	prod	☐
13	drip	☐	38	prop	☐
14	drop	☐	39	snag	☐
15	drum	☐	40	snap	☐
16	dry	☐	41	snip	☐
17	flag	☐	42	snob	☐
18	flan	☐	43	snub	☐
19	flap	☐	44	snug	☐
20	flat	☐	45	swag	☐
21	flax	☐	46	swam	☐
22	fled	☐	47	swig	☐
23	flop	☐	48	swim	☐
24	glad	☐	49	Switzerland	☐
25	gland	☐	50	swum	☐

WORD LIST 5

1	brew	☐	26	spring	☐
2	brim	☐	27	sprint	☐
3	brusque	☐	28	stab	☐
4	scamp	☐	29	stag	☐
5	scan	☐	30	stamp	☐
6	scram	☐	31	stanza	☐
7	scrap	☐	32	steeple-jack	☐
8	scrimp	☐	33	stem	☐
9	script	☐	34	step	☐
10	scrub	☐	35	stilt	☐
11	scrum	☐	36	sting	☐
12	scum	☐	37	stop	☐
13	shred	☐	38	strand	☐
14	shrift	☐	39	strap	☐
15	shrimp	☐	40	strip	☐
16	shrink	☐	41	strong	☐
17	shrivel	☐	42	strongbox	☐
18	shrub	☐	43	strum	☐
19	shrug	☐	44	strung	☐
20	splash	☐	45	strut	☐
21	splint	☐	46	stub	☐
22	split	☐	47	stud	☐
23	sprang	☐	48	stump	☐
24	sprat	☐	49	stunt	☐
25	sprig	☐	50	sty	☐

WORD LIST 6

1	bath	☐	26	rash	☐
2	bunch	☐	27	rich	☐
3	cash	☐	28	ring	☐
4	chat	☐	29	sang	☐
5	chin	☐	30	shed	☐
6	chip	☐	31	ship	☐
7	chop	☐	32	shop	☐
8	dish	☐	33	shut	☐
9	father	☐	34	sing	☐
10	fish	☐	35	song	☐
11	hush	☐	36	that	☐
12	inch	☐	37	the	☐
13	Joshua	☐	38	theft	☐
14	king	☐	39	them	☐
15	long	☐	40	then	☐
16	lunch	☐	41	thin	☐
17	lung	☐	42	thing	☐
18	mixing	☐	43	this	☐
19	moth	☐	44	thud	☐
20	mother	☐	45	Thursday	☐
21	munch	☐	46	vanish	☐
22	path	☐	47	wing	☐
23	pinch	☐	48	wish	☐
24	quench	☐	49	with	☐
25	rang	☐	50	zither	☐

WORD LIST 7

1	any	☐	26	seven	☐
2	are	☐	27	should	☐
3	beautiful	☐	28	some	☐
4	because	☐	29	their	☐
5	come	☐	30	there	☐
6	could	☐	31	they	☐
7	do	☐	32	three	☐
8	does	☐	33	toes	☐
9	eight	☐	34	too	☐
10	for	☐	35	two	☐
11	four	☐	36	tzar	☐
12	friend	☐	37	want	☐
13	give	☐	38	was	☐
14	have	☐	39	were	☐
15	island	☐	40	what	☐
16	juice	☐	41	when	☐
17	key	☐	42	where	☐
18	many	☐	43	which	☐
19	of	☐	44	who	☐
20	once	☐	45	why	☐
21	one	☐	46	witch	☐
22	put	☐	47	would	☐
23	query	☐	48	xylophone	☐
24	said	☐	49	you	☐
25	saw	☐	50	your	☐

WORD LIST 8

1	ass	☐	26 kill	☐
2	bill	☐	27 kiss	☐
3	buzz	☐	28 less	☐
4	candy-floss	☐	29 loss	☐
5	chess	☐	30 mess	☐
6	class	☐	31 mill	☐
7	cliff	☐	32 miss	☐
8	cross	☐	33 moss	☐
9	cuff	☐	34 off	☐
10	doll	☐	35 overspill	☐
11	dress	☐	36 press	☐
12	drill	☐	37 puff	☐
13	express	☐	38 quell	☐
14	fluff	☐	39 shall	☐
15	frill	☐	40 shell	☐
16	frizz	☐	41 shrill	☐
17	glass	☐	42 snuff	☐
18	gloss	☐	43 spell	☐
19	grill	☐	44 spill	☐
20	gruff	☐	45 stiff	☐
21	gull	☐	46 still	☐
22	hill	☐	47 stress	☐
23	hiss	☐	48 swell	☐
24	hull	☐	49 toss	☐
25	jazz	☐	50 whizz	☐

WORD LIST 9

1	barn	☐	26	jerk	☐
2	birch	☐	27	lark	☐
3	bird	☐	28	lurch	☐
4	born	☐	29	over	☐
5	burn	☐	30	perm	☐
6	burst	☐	31	porch	☐
7	cart	☐	32	port	☐
8	charm	☐	33	quirk	☐
9	chart	☐	34	scarf	☐
10	chirp	☐	35	sharp	☐
11	church	☐	36	slur	☐
12	churn	☐	37	smart	☐
13	corn	☐	38	sort	☐
14	curl	☐	39	sport	☐
15	darn	☐	40	spurt	☐
16	dirt	☐	41	start	☐
17	exert	☐	42	stern	☐
18	farm	☐	43	stir	☐
19	fern	☐	44	surf	☐
20	firm	☐	45	term	☐
21	first	☐	46	third	☐
22	girl	☐	47	torn	☐
23	harsh	☐	48	worn	☐
24	her	☐	49	yarn	☐
25	horn	☐	50	zero	☐

WORD LIST 10

1	admit	☐	26	lemon	☐
2	antic	☐	27	lily	☐
3	bandit	☐	28	magnet	☐
4	basket	☐	29	metric	☐
5	bitter	☐	30	nutmeg	☐
6	brandish	☐	31	oblong	☐
7	carpet	☐	32	optic	☐
8	cobweb	☐	33	picnic	☐
9	combat	☐	34	piglet	☐
10	conduct	☐	35	problem	☐
11	confess	☐	36	quintet	☐
12	contact	☐	37	robin	☐
13	contest	☐	38	rustic	☐
14	convict	☐	39	selfish	☐
15	dentist	☐	40	silver	☐
16	fabric	☐	41	splendid	☐
17	garden	☐	42	sunset	☐
18	goblin	☐	43	tablet	☐
19	hatbox	☐	44	tactic	☐
20	helmet	☐	45	tartan	☐
21	hotpot	☐	46	tractor	☐
22	humbug	☐	47	triplet	☐
23	inject	☐	48	victim	☐
24	inland	☐	49	wigwam	☐
25	insect	☐	50	zigzag	☐

WORD LIST 11

1	adder	☐	26	lesson	☐
2	adding	☐	27	letter	☐
3	batter	☐	28	matter	☐
4	batting	☐	29	mitten	☐
5	better	☐	30	otter	☐
6	blotter	☐	31	pepper	☐
7	butter	☐	32	pillow	☐
8	button	☐	33	potter	☐
9	cannot	☐	34	quitter	☐
10	carrot	☐	35	ribbon	☐
11	chatter	☐	36	robber	☐
12	copper	☐	37	rubber	☐
13	cotton	☐	38	shatter	☐
14	dagger	☐	39	slipper	☐
15	digger	☐	40	stagger	☐
16	dinner	☐	41	suffix	☐
17	fellow	☐	42	summer	☐
18	fitting	☐	43	supper	☐
19	flatten	☐	44	tennis	☐
20	flatter	☐	45	upper	☐
21	hammer	☐	46	villa	☐
22	horrid	☐	47	wedding	☐
23	inner	☐	48	winner	☐
24	judder	☐	49	yellow	☐
25	kipper	☐	50	zipper	☐

WORD LIST 12

1	bake	☐	26	mine	☐
2	bone	☐	27	mistake	☐
3	cake	☐	28	pale	☐
4	compete	☐	29	quake	☐
5	complete	☐	30	quote	☐
6	compute	☐	31	rake	☐
7	concrete	☐	32	ride	☐
8	cube	☐	33	safe	☐
9	date	☐	34	save	☐
10	dispute	☐	35	shake	☐
11	dive	☐	36	side	☐
12	explode	☐	37	slope	☐
13	fate	☐	38	strike	☐
14	five	☐	39	take	☐
15	flute	☐	40	tame	☐
16	froze	☐	41	these	☐
17	gale	☐	42	tide	☐
18	gaze	☐	43	time	☐
19	hole	☐	44	tube	☐
20	hope	☐	45	tune	☐
21	joke	☐	46	vine	☐
22	lake	☐	47	wake	☐
23	lane	☐	48	wife	☐
24	late	☐	49	wine	☐
25	like	☐	50	yoke	☐

WORD LIST 13

1	afternoon	☐	26	keep	☐
2	agree	☐	27	knee	☐
3	aloof	☐	28	look	☐
4	bee	☐	29	mood	☐
5	been	☐	30	moon	☐
6	book	☐	31	proof	☐
7	breeze	☐	32	queen	☐
8	cheese	☐	33	rook	☐
9	choose	☐	34	room	☐
10	cook	☐	35	school	☐
11	cuckoo	☐	36	screech	☐
12	deep	☐	37	see	☐
13	exceed	☐	38	seventeen	☐
14	feed	☐	39	shook	☐
15	feet	☐	40	sleepy	☐
16	food	☐	41	sleeve	☐
17	foolish	☐	42	smooth	☐
18	free	☐	43	spoon	☐
19	freedom	☐	44	squeeze	☐
20	freeze	☐	45	sweet	☐
21	good	☐	46	teeth	☐
22	goose	☐	47	took	☐
23	green		48	tooth	☐
24	hook	☐	49	wood	☐
25	jeep	☐	50	zoom	☐

WORD LIST 14

1	Atlantic	☐	26	ketchup	☐
2	attack	☐	27	kitten	☐
3	back	☐	28	lock	☐
4	bank	☐	29	locket	☐
5	brick	☐	30	magic	☐
6	bucket	☐	31	milk	☐
7	cabin	☐	32	Pacific	☐
8	cactus	☐	33	panic	☐
9	calendar	☐	34	pink	☐
10	camera	☐	35	plastic	☐
11	canal	☐	36	pocket	☐
12	check	☐	37	quick	☐
13	clinic	☐	38	rink	☐
14	colonize	☐	39	rock	☐
15	corner	☐	40	septic	☐
16	drink	☐	41	silk	☐
17	elastic	☐	42	sink	☐
18	fantastic	☐	43	sock	☐
19	folk	☐	44	static	☐
20	frantic	☐	45	tank	☐
21	havoc	☐	46	toxic	☐
22	hectic	☐	47	trunk	☐
23	junk	☐	48	wicket	☐
24	keen	☐	49	wink	☐
25	kennel	☐	50	yolk	☐

WORD LIST 15

#	Word		#	Word	
1	absence	☐	26	lease	☐
2	abyss	☐	27	lice	☐
3	ace	☐	28	loose	☐
4	acquaintance	☐	29	mass	☐
5	across	☐	30	moose	☐
6	address	☐	31	nice	☐
7	advice	☐	32	notice	☐
8	boss	☐	33	office	☐
9	chase	☐	34	peace	☐
10	confuse	☐	35	piece	☐
11	difference	☐	36	place	☐
12	distress	☐	37	police	☐
13	dose	☐	38	practice	☐
14	existence	☐	39	practise	☐
15	fleece	☐	40	price	☐
16	France	☐	41	prince	☐
17	fuss	☐	42	reduce	☐
18	grace	☐	43	release	☐
19	happiness	☐	44	rice	☐
20	house	☐	45	sentence	☐
21	ice	☐	46	service	☐
22	justice	☐	47	since	☐
23	kindliness	☐	48	spice	☐
24	lace	☐	49	trace	☐
25	laziness		50	twice	☐

WORD LIST 16

1	angle	☐	26	needle	☐
2	apple	☐	27	noble	☐
3	battle	☐	28	paddle	☐
4	bristle	☐	29	pebble	☐
5	bubble	☐	30	poodle	☐
6	castle	☐	31	purple	☐
7	cradle	☐	32	puzzle	☐
8	cuddle	☐	33	quibble	☐
9	dazzle	☐	34	rattle	☐
10	duffle	☐	35	rifle	☐
11	dwindle	☐	36	rustle	☐
12	eagle	☐	37	saddle	☐
13	example	☐	38	shingle	☐
14	fiddle	☐	39	simple	☐
15	giggle	☐	40	single	☐
16	gobble	☐	41	smuggle	☐
17	hobble	☐	42	snuffle	☐
18	hurdle	☐	43	table	☐
19	idle	☐	44	thistle	☐
20	invisible	☐	45	title	☐
21	jumble	☐	46	triangle	☐
22	kettle	☐	47	trifle	☐
23	ladle	☐	48	whistle	☐
24	meddle	☐	49	wrestle	☐
25	muddle	☐	50	yaffle	☐

WORD LIST 17

1	ankle	☐	26	particle	☐
2	article	☐	27	physical	☐
3	barnacle	☐	28	pickle	☐
4	bicycle	☐	29	pinnacle	☐
5	buckle	☐	30	political	☐
6	cackle	☐	31	practical	☐
7	chronicle	☐	32	prickle	☐
8	chuckle	☐	33	quizzical	☐
9	classical	☐	34	radical	☐
10	crackle	☐	35	sparkle	☐
11	crinkle	☐	36	speckle	☐
12	cubicle	☐	37	spectacle	☐
13	cuticle	☐	38	sprinkle	☐
14	electrical	☐	39	tackle	☐
15	extraphysical	☐	40	technical	☐
16	freckle	☐	41	tentacle	☐
17	heckle	☐	42	tickle	☐
18	identical	☐	43	topical	☐
19	juridical	☐	44	trickle	☐
20	magical	☐	45	tropical	☐
21	manacle	☐	46	twinkle	☐
22	musical	☐	47	vehicle	☐
23	nautical	☐	48	winkle	☐
24	obstacle	☐	49	wrinkle	☐
25	oracle	☐	50	zoological	☐

WORD LIST 18

1	afraid	☐	26	nail	☐
2	again	☐	27	obtain	☐
3	against	☐	28	pain	☐
4	betray	☐	29	plaice	☐
5	birthday	☐	30	portrait	☐
6	brain	☐	31	quail	☐
7	castaway	☐	32	rain	☐
8	chain	☐	33	raise	☐
9	complain	☐	34	remain	☐
10	contain	☐	35	say	☐
11	decay	☐	36	snail	☐
12	delay	☐	37	Spain	☐
13	dismay	☐	38	spray	☐
14	display	☐	39	stay	☐
15	drain	☐	40	stowaway	☐
16	entertain	☐	41	stray	☐
17	explain	☐	42	tail	☐
18	faint	☐	43	today	☐
19	grain	☐	44	trail	☐
20	haystack	☐	45	train	☐
21	holiday	☐	46	unafraid	☐
22	jail	☐	47	vain	☐
23	maize	☐	48	waist	☐
24	midday	☐	49	wait	☐
25	motorway	☐	50	yesterday	☐

WORD LIST 19

1	about	☐	26	hoax	☐
2	allow	☐	27	jowl	☐
3	aloud	☐	28	know	☐
4	aquashow	☐	29	moat	☐
5	around	☐	30	mountain	☐
6	bellow	☐	31	mouse	☐
7	bowl	☐	32	mouth	☐
8	brown	☐	33	ounce	☐
9	cloud	☐	34	outsize	☐
10	clown	☐	35	owl	☐
11	coax	☐	36	power	☐
12	county	☐	37	road	☐
13	crow	☐	38	roast	☐
14	discount	☐	39	scarecrow	☐
15	elbow	☐	40	scowl	☐
16	float	☐	41	shallow	☐
17	follow	☐	42	shower	☐
18	found	☐	43	thousand	☐
19	frown	☐	44	throat	☐
20	glow	☐	45	throw	☐
21	goal	☐	46	tower	☐
22	goat	☐	47	town	☐
23	groan	☐	48	trousers	☐
24	grow	☐	49	trout	☐
25	growl	☐	50	vow	☐

WORD LIST 20

1	beach	☐	26	jealousy	☐
2	bread	☐	27	mean	☐
3	break	☐	28	peach	☐
4	breakage	☐	29	pheasant	☐
5	breakdown	☐	30	pleasant	☐
6	breath	☐	31	please	☐
7	breathe	☐	32	pleasure	☐
8	cheat	☐	33	reason	☐
9	colleague	☐	34	reveal	☐
10	crease	☐	35	scream	☐
11	creature	☐	36	speak	☐
12	deaf	☐	37	spread	☐
13	disease	☐	38	squeak	☐
14	dreadful	☐	39	steady	☐
15	dream	☐	40	steak	☐
16	each	☐	41	stealth	☐
17	feather	☐	42	stream	☐
18	flea	☐	43	teacher	☐
19	grease	☐	44	thread	☐
20	great	☐	45	treachery	☐
21	greatly	☐	46	tread	☐
22	Greatorex	☐	47	treasure	☐
23	health	☐	48	wealth	☐
24	heaven	☐	49	yeast	☐
25	instead	☐	50	zealous	☐

WORD LIST 21

1	applause	☐	26	haunted	☐
2	astronaut	☐	27	hawk	☐
3	audience	☐	28	hawthorn	☐
4	August	☐	29	jaunty	☐
5	awful	☐	30	jaw	☐
6	awkward	☐	31	jigsaw	☐
7	awning	☐	32	launch	☐
8	bauble	☐	33	laundry	☐
9	bawl	☐	34	law	☐
10	cause	☐	35	lawn	☐
11	caustic	☐	36	pauper	☐
12	caution	☐	37	pause	☐
13	claw	☐	38	pawn	☐
14	crawl	☐	39	raucous	☐
15	daunted	☐	40	raw	☐
16	dawdle	☐	41	sauce	☐
17	dawn	☐	42	saucer	☐
18	draw	☐	43	saunter	☐
19	exhausted	☐	44	squaw	☐
20	fault	☐	45	squawk	☐
21	gauze	☐	46	straw	☐
22	gnaw	☐	47	taunt	☐
23	haulage	☐	48	tawdry	☐
24	haulier	☐	49	traumatic	☐
25	haunt	☐	50	vault	☐

WORD LIST 22

1	argue	☐	26	knew	☐
2	avenue	☐	27	mildew	☐
3	barbecue	☐	28	neurology	☐
4	blew	☐	29	neurotic	☐
5	blue	☐	30	neutral	☐
6	chew	☐	31	new	☐
7	clue	☐	32	newt	☐
8	continue	☐	33	pew	☐
9	corkscrew	☐	34	pharmaceutical	☐
10	crew	☐	35	pneumonia	☐
11	curlew	☐	36	queue	☐
12	deuce	☐	37	renew	☐
13	dew	☐	38	rheumatism	☐
14	drew	☐	39	shrewd	☐
15	due	☐	40	sleuth	☐
16	eucalyptus	☐	41	statue	☐
17	eureka	☐	42	stew	☐
18	Europe	☐	43	subdue	☐
19	eutaxia	☐	44	therapeutic	☐
20	feud	☐	45	threw	☐
21	few	☐	46	tissue	☐
22	flew	☐	47	true	☐
23	glue	☐	48	value	☐
24	grew	☐	49	yew	☐
25	jewel	☐	50	Zeus	☐

WORD LIST 23

1	adjective	☐	26	January	☐
2	badge	☐	27	joking	☐
3	barge	☐	28	jonquil	☐
4	bridge	☐	29	joyful	☐
5	cage	☐	30	jubilant	☐
6	dodge	☐	31	judge	☐
7	drudge	☐	32	July	☐
8	edge	☐	33	June	☐
9	fudge	☐	34	jury	☐
10	gem	☐	35	just	☐
11	general	☐	36	juxtapose	☐
12	generalization	☐	37	large	☐
13	genius	☐	38	ledge	☐
14	gentle	☐	39	lodge	☐
15	geography	☐	40	luggage	☐
16	German	☐	41	object	☐
17	giant	☐	42	page	☐
18	ginger	☐	43	plunge	☐
19	giraffe	☐	44	rage	☐
20	grudge	☐	45	ridge	☐
21	gymnastics	☐	46	sage	☐
22	hedge	☐	47	smudge	☐
23	hinge	☐	48	subject	☐
24	huge	☐	49	wage	☐
25	injection	☐	50	wedge	☐

WORD LIST 24

1	alphabet	☐	26 Joseph	☐
2	apostrophe	☐	27 offer	☐
3	autobiography	☐	28 orphan	☐
4	autograph	☐	29 paragraph	☐
5	buffalo	☐	30 phantom	☐
6	catastrophe	☐	31 pharmacist	☐
7	coffee	☐	32 pharmacy	☐
8	curfew	☐	33 phenomenal	☐
9	daffodil	☐	34 philosophy	☐
10	different	☐	35 photocopy	☐
11	dolphin	☐	36 photograph	☐
12	emphasis	☐	37 photography	☐
13	factory	☐	38 physics	☐
14	failure	☐	39 physique	☐
15	faithfully	☐	40 profit	☐
16	fanatic	☐	41 prophet	☐
17	farther	☐	42 radiography	☐
18	fatigue	☐	43 sphere	☐
19	favourite	☐	44 suffer	☐
20	February	☐	45 sulphur	☐
21	fickle	☐	46 telegraph	☐
22	fierce	☐	47 telephone	☐
23	fixture	☐	48 toffee	☐
24	fizz	☐	49 traffic	☐
25	furious	☐	50 triumph	☐

WORD LIST 25

1	ambitious	☐	26	joyous	☐
2	anxious	☐	27	luxurious	☐
3	bonus	☐	28	marvellous	☐
4	cantankerous	☐	29	monotonous	☐
5	cautious	☐	30	mountainous	☐
6	census	☐	31	mysterious	☐
7	circus	☐	32	nervous	☐
8	conscious	☐	33	numerous	☐
9	contagious	☐	34	obvious	☐
10	courageous	☐	35	perilous	☐
11	crocus	☐	36	poisonous	☐
12	dangerous	☐	37	precious	☐
13	delicious	☐	38	querulous	☐
14	enormous	☐	39	ruinous	☐
15	fabulous	☐	40	serious	☐
16	famous	☐	41	spacious	☐
17	fictitious	☐	42	status	☐
18	focus	☐	43	suspicious	☐
19	fungus	☐	44	tedious	☐
20	generous	☐	45	terminus	☐
21	glorious	☐	46	thunderous	☐
22	gracious	☐	47	tremendous	☐
23	hazardous	☐	48	victorious	☐
24	humorous	☐	49	virus	☐
25	jealous	☐	50	wondrous	☐

WORD LIST 26

1	aggravation	☐	26 inspection	☐
2	aggression	☐	27 juxtaposition	☐
3	attention	☐	28 lotion	☐
4	beautician	☐	29 magician	☐
5	completion	☐	30 motion	☐
6	comprehension	☐	31 musician	☐
7	compulsion	☐	32 nation	☐
8	condition	☐	33 optician	☐
9	depression	☐	34 permission	☐
10	dictation	☐	35 politician	☐
11	discussion	☐	36 population	☐
12	distraction	☐	37 procession	☐
13	diversion	☐	38 profession	☐
14	electrician	☐	39 propulsion	☐
15	embarkation	☐	40 realization	☐
16	examination	☐	41 recognition	☐
17	expression	☐	42 session	☐
18	fixation	☐	43 situation	☐
19	gyration	☐	44 submersion	☐
20	ignition	☐	45 superstition	☐
21	immersion	☐	46 taxation	☐
22	imposition	☐	47 technician	☐
23	impression	☐	48 tuition	☐
24	innovation	☐	49 vacation	☐
25	inquisition	☐	50 workstation	☐

WORD LIST 27

1	ache	☐	26	library	☐
2	already	☐	27	meant	☐
3	answer	☐	28	minute	☐
4	apparatus	☐	29	mystery	☐
5	beginning	☐	30	necessary	☐
6	believe	☐	31	nephew	☐
7	business	☐	32	niece	☐
8	colour	☐	33	parliament	☐
9	cough	☐	34	people	☐
10	course	☐	35	pigeon	☐
11	cushion	☐	36	quiet	☐
12	doctor	☐	37	quite	☐
13	enough	☐	38	receive	☐
14	eventually	☐	39	rhyme	☐
15	exaggerate	☐	40	rhythm	☐
16	exhibition	☐	41	right	☐
17	fascinate	☐	42	separate	☐
18	foreign	☐	43	sincerely	☐
19	government	☐	44	special	☐
20	grammar	☐	45	successful	☐
21	guess	☐	46	temperature	☐
22	immediately	☐	47	weather	☐
23	jewellery	☐	48	whether	☐
24	judgement	☐	49	write	☐
25	knowledge	☐	50	zoology	☐

www.ingramcontent.com/pod-product-compliance
Lightning Source LLC
Chambersburg PA
CBHW081635040426

42449CB00014B/3320